BIBLEFORCE®

THE FIRST HEROES
DEVOTIONAL

To:

_____

From:

_____

Date:

_____

Estimada y queridisima
    Nadia.

Tu eres una chispa de Alegria.
Tienes un corazon hermoso.
Que Nadie y Nada te robe lo
Bello de tu corazon.

Recive este maravilloso libro,
donde encontras historias que
te ayudaran hacer una Niña
Inteligente, Amorosa, Respetosa y
Sobre Todo llena del Amor De

Dios.

Si tu estudias este libro tan maravilloso,
vas a encontrar tesoros que te ayudaran
todo la Vida.
Este es nuestro deceo para Ti:

    Con Mucho Cariño y Amor.
Shiloh, Massimo y Antonella
        Dios te bendiga
        TODOS los dias De tu
    Vida.

05.08.24.

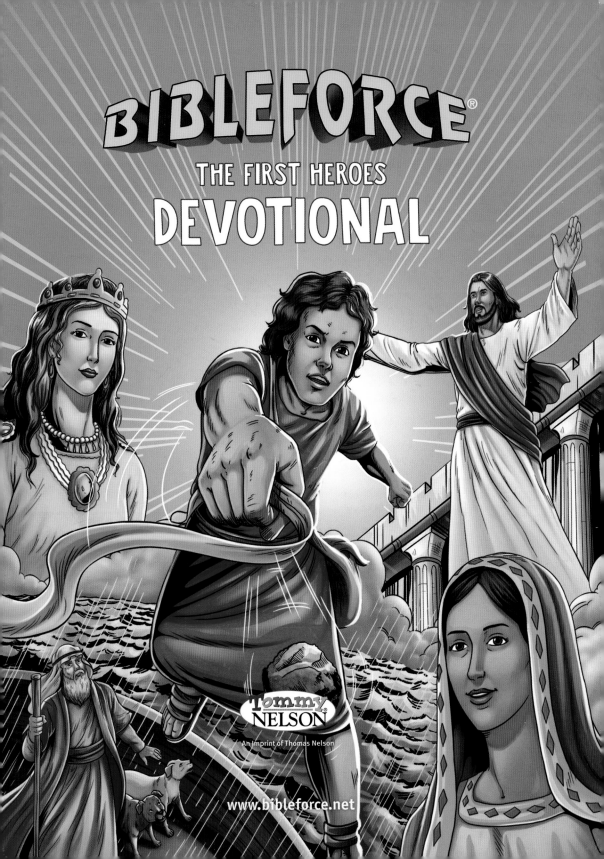

BibleForce® Devotional: The First Heroes Devotional
Copyright © 2019 by North Parade Publishing Ltd. and International Publishing Services Pty Ltd.

North Parade Publishing
4 North Parade, Bath BA1 1LF, United Kingdom
www.nppbooks.co.uk

International Publishing Services Pty Ltd.
Sydney, Australia
www.ipsoz.com

BibleForce® was created by Wayne McKay and Peter Hicks.
BibleForce® is a wholly owned registered trademark of International Publishing Services, Sydney, Australia.

Publishers: Wayne McKay and Peter Hicks.
Consulting Author and General Editor: Janice Emmerson
Editorial Team: Mark Friedman, John Perritano, and Fraser Emmerson-Hicks
Design Team: Directed by Janice Emmerson

Published in Nashville, Tennessee, by Tommy Nelson. Tommy Nelson is an imprint of Thomas Nelson. Thomas Nelson is a registered trademark of HarperCollins Christian Publishing, Inc.

Written by Tama Fortner.

Tommy Nelson titles may be purchased in bulk for educational, business, fund-raising, or sales promotional use. For information, please email SpecialMarkets@ThomasNelson.com.

Library of Congress Cataloging-in-Publication Data
Names: Fortner, Tama, 1969- author.
Title: *BibleForce® Devotional: The First Heroes Devotional* written by Tama Fortner.
Description: Nashville : Thomas Nelson, 2019.
Identifiers: LCCN 2018052103 | ISBN 9781400212637 (hardcover)
Subjects: LCSH: Heroes in the Bible--Juvenile literature. | Devotional literature--Juvenile literature. | Children--Prayers and devotions.
Classification: LCC BS579.H4 F67 2019 | DDC 242/.62--dc23 LC record available at https://lccn.loc.gov/2018052103
ISBN-13: 978-1-4002-1263-7

Printed in Hong Kong

19 20 21 22 23 IPS 6 5 4 3 2 1

Mfr: Dragon Sourcing (Far East) Ltd. / Chai Wan, Hong Kong / July 2019 / PO #9519316

"I tell you the truth, anyone who believes in me will do the same works I have done, and even greater works."

—JOHN 14:12 NLT

Contents

New Testament

Introduction

What Is a Hero?

I n today's world, the word *hero* gets tossed around a lot, and the image that pops into your mind is probably a pretty epic one. Thanks to comic books and movies, you might imagine someone flying around in a cape or an invisible airplane. Or you might picture someone who swoops into impossible situations to save the day with superhuman strength. But in real life, heroes are ordinary people, just like you.

When you first read about the heroes of the Bible, it's easy to think they were all somehow extraordinary and that's why they were able to do such amazing and memorable things. But as you learn more about them, you'll find that they were really quite ordinary people—shepherds and tentmakers and housewives. Yes, there was a queen and even a king or two, but even they were far from perfect. The thing that made them heroes wasn't superhuman strength or even superhuman faith. They became heroes because they chose to love and live for an extraordinary God. And that's something anyone can do.

When you put your faith in God, you can make a difference. Those caped heroes of your imagination might help save lives, but as a hero of the faith, you can help save souls by shining the light of God into the darkness of the world.

SO . . . WHAT IS BIBLEFORCE®?

BibleForce is all the action and excitement of God's truth captured in the pages of a book and made real for readers just like you. The journey begins with *BibleForce: The First Heroes Bible*. This Bible storybook is illustrated like a graphic novel, and the heroes of the Old and New Testaments leap to life in action-packed art, while the stories encourage you to dive into the real-life adventures of the Bible. With nearly two hundred amazing and heroic stories, it's a book you won't want to put down.

THE BIBLEFORCE DEVOTIONAL

The excitement continues with the *BibleForce Devotional: The First Heroes Devotional.* In this book, you can dig deeper and learn more about the greatest heroes of the Bible. Each of the one hundred devotions connects the events that shaped these heroes' lives to situations that you might face in your own life. As you discover how Bible heroes handled their troubles, you'll learn to better handle the tough stuff that comes your way—and faithfully follow God at the same time. This book is also full of fun facts and activities that will make your time with God even more exciting.

Fun Facts

Each devotion begins with some **Fun Facts** about the hero or Bible story. You'll learn things like when and where heroes lived, who their families were, and how God used them. These facts will give you a bigger picture of who each hero really was: an ordinary person—very much like you—who was willing to be used by our extraordinary God.

> ALSO KNOWN AS: DORCAS
>
> WHERE: THE CITY OF JOPPA, IN ISRAEL
>
> KNOWN FOR: ALWAYS DOING GOOD AND HELPING THE POOR

Hero Training

> 🏃 HERO TRAINING Part of growing up is figuring out who you are. The world will tell you all sorts of things—things that aren't true. Always turn to God to find out who you really are. Start with these beautiful verses: 1 John 3:1, Galatians 4:7, Psalm 139:13–14, and 1 Peter 2:9.

Even heroes need to train! In **Hero Training** you'll increase your Bible knowledge by looking up different Scripture passages to learn more about God's truth and promises. With questions that make you think, **Hero Training** will strengthen your mental muscles and faith muscles as you learn to apply the words of the Bible to your own life.

Be a Hero!

By now you know that faith isn't just about what you know; it's about what you do. That's why each **Be a Hero!** excercise will challenge you to live out what you've learned. Filled with ideas, fun activities, and everyday opportunities for you to put your faith into action, **Be a Hero!** will help you become the real-life hero God created you to be.

BE A HERO!

When Jesus scooped up those children, they must have been given the world's best hug! Your hugs are pretty powerful too. They can say, "I love you," "I'm sorry," and "I'm here for you." Be a hero and hug a friend in need today!

With their can't-put-down stories and action-packed art, *BibleForce: The First Heroes Bible* and *BibleForce Devotional* will not only help you understand what it means to be one of God's heroes, but they'll also help you become a real-life hero of faith.

A Flood of Trouble

Noah—The Last Good Man

"Don't be afraid, because I have saved you. I have called you by name, and you are mine. When you pass through the waters, I will be with you."

—ISAIAH 43:1-2 ICB

FATHER: LAMECH

SONS: SHEM, HAM, AND JAPHETH

LIFE SPAN: DIED AT AGE 950

Have you been stuck in a maze? Perhaps it was a corn maze or one of those carnival mirror mazes. No matter which way you turned, you found a dead end. Then, just as you were about to give up, you heard a familiar voice—*Dad!* You knew he'd take care of you because you belong to him.

God also takes care of those who belong to Him, who love and follow Him. In the days of Noah, not many people followed God. In fact, Noah was the only man in the whole world who still loved God. So when God told him a terrible flood was coming to destroy every living creature on earth, Noah might have thought that was a dead end for him. But it wasn't. God told Noah to build an ark—a boat big enough to hold him, his family, and two of every animal on earth. Noah did exactly as God said. And all throughout the forty days and nights of rain, God kept Noah and all those inside the ark safe.

When you're facing a flood of trouble and there seems to be no way out, remember that God saves those who belong to Him. Love God, trust Him, and follow Him even when you don't yet see the way out. And He will take care of you. ▶ *GENESIS 6–8*

🏃 **HERO TRAINING** Noah must have had a terrifying ride inside that ark! When you're frightened, remember Isaiah 43:1–2. Claim this promise by making it your own: *God saves me. He calls me by my name. I belong to Him. He will always be with me.*

👤 BE A HERO!

You may not be able to save the way God does, but you can save the day—or at least someone's day. Be alert for opportunities. Whose day can you "save" with a helping hand, a kind word, a great big hug, or a listening ear?

GOD SAVED EVERYONE ON THE ARK.

3

Abraham—The Chosen One

WHO: ABRAHAM; HIS WIFE, SARAH; AND HIS NEPHEW, LOT

ANCESTOR: NOAH

WHERE: HARAN, A CITY IN MESOPOTAMIA; IN PRESENT-DAY TURKEY

AGE: ABRAHAM WAS 75 YEARS OLD WHEN HE LEFT HARAN

If you go the wrong way . . . you will hear a voice behind you. It will say, "This is the right way. You should go this way."

—ISAIAH 30:21 ICB

ABRAHAM HAD GREAT FAITH IN GOD. HE SET OUT FOR THE PROMISED LAND WITH HIS WIFE AND HIS NEPHEW, LOT.

When you and your family want to take a trip, the first thing you probably do is decide where to go. After all, how can you go somewhere without knowing where that somewhere is?

Abraham probably wondered where his somewhere was when God spoke to him and said, "Go." But God didn't give any details. He just said, "Take your family. Go to the land I will show you."

You see, God had chosen Abraham to be the father of His people. But Abraham and his wife, Sarah, didn't have any children. And they had already grown old. So when God promised to make a great nation of Abraham's family, it was hard to believe. But Abraham believed God anyway. And even though he didn't know where God was leading him, Abraham packed up. He took his family—his wife, Sarah, and his nephew, Lot—and followed God.

As you learn to follow God, there will be times when you're not sure where He's leading you. Trust Him anyway. He'll show you each new step to take, and He'll walk with you the whole way. ▶GENESIS 12

✝ BE A HERO!

Following God can be hard, but it's easier with a friend. Read Ecclesiastes 4:9–10. How can you help a friend follow God today? Pray together. Talk about your troubles together. And always stand by each other.

☆ HERO TRAINING Abraham could have made up excuses not to go. He could have said, "I'm seventy-five years old!" or "I like my home in Haran." But he didn't. Are you making excuses for not following God—for not loving your neighbor, forgiving a friend, or reading the Bible? Decide to stop making excuses and do what God says!

Believing Anyway

Abraham—Who Believed God's Promise

LOOK UP IN THE NIGHT SKY. COUNT THE STARS. JUST AS THE STARS ARE MANY, SO WILL YOUR DESCENDANTS BE.

MEANING OF NAME: "FATHER OF MANY PEOPLE"

ALSO KNOWN AS: ABRAM, MEANING "GREAT FATHER"; GOD CHANGED ABRAM'S NAME TO ABRAHAM WHEN HE WAS 99 YEARS OLD

WHERE: CANAAN, ALSO CALLED THE PROMISED LAND; NOW PART OF THE COUNTRIES OF LEBANON, SYRIA, JORDAN, AND ISRAEL

Faith means knowing that something is real even if we do not see it.

—HEBREWS 11:1 ICB

Have you ever had to wait for a promise to be kept? Perhaps you were promised a trip to go sledding or camping, but you had to wait until the weather was right. Even when you know a promised thing is coming, waiting is so hard!

What if you had to wait for years? How hard would it be to keep believing in the promise? When God told Abraham to leave his home, God promised to make his family into a great nation—even though Abraham had no children. Years later, after Abraham and Sarah reached Canaan (the land God sent them to), they were still childless. But God said, "I will give this land to you and all your offspring." Still later, God told Abraham to count the stars: "Just as the stars are many, so will your descendants be."

Abraham didn't have one child, much less a whole starry sky's worth. It seemed impossible, but Abraham believed anyway. He didn't know how or when, but he had faith that God would keep His promise. And God blessed him for that faith.

The Bible is filled with God's promises to you. You may not understand how or when God will keep those promises, but believe Him anyway—even when the wait is hard. You'll see those promises fulfilled. ▶ *GENESIS 12, 15*

BE A HERO!

Our faith in God is what saves us, but if our "faith does nothing, then that faith is dead" (James 2:17 ICB). So show that your faith in God and His love is alive! Without saying a word, how many ways can you show others that God loves them today?

🏃 **HERO TRAINING** Hebrews 11 is often called the "Hall of Faith." Read this chapter about the many heroes of the faith. Who is your favorite? Dig a little deeper into the Bible and find out more about his or her story and faith.

A Promise Kept

Sarah—The Joyful

MEANING OF NAME: "PRINCESS"

ALSO KNOWN AS: SARAI, MEANING "PRINCESS" (OR, PERHAPS, "QUARRELSOME")

HUSBAND: ABRAHAM

AGE: 90 YEARS OLD WHEN ISAAC WAS BORN

It was by faith that even Sarah was able to have a child. . . . She believed that God would keep his promise.

—HEBREWS 11:11 NLT

Think about what fills you with joy—not the things that give you a quick smile but those things that fill you with warmth for days. Perhaps it's the way your mom hugs you so tight or the way your dad cheers the loudest for you.

The things that bring the greatest joy aren't things you can buy in a store. They're blessings straight from God. Sarah waited a long time for her blessing of joy. God had promised her a son, but it had been so long that she had almost given up hope. In fact, when she overheard the Lord again promising Abraham a son, she laughed! After all, over two decades had passed. She was now an old woman—far too old to have a son.

But despite her laughter, Sarah did hope and believe. And nine months later, she did have a son, just as God promised. She and Abraham named him Isaac, which means "laughter." God kept His promise and blessed Sarah with great joy.

Sarah found God's promise a bit hard to believe at first. But she eventually had faith that God had a special plan for her and Abraham through the blessing of a baby boy. God kept His promise to Sarah and Abraham. He will keep every promise He makes to you too! And seeing those promises come true will give you the greatest joy of all. ▶ GENESIS 18, 21

☠ BE A HERO!

You can trust God to keep every promise He makes. Would people say the same thing about you? Heroes do what they say they will do. Did you promise to take out the trash or help clean out the garage? Then go do it! Always keep your promises.

🏃 HERO TRAINING There are 5,467 promises from God in the Bible. And God has kept—and is still keeping—every single one. How many promises can you find? Here are some to get you started: 1 John 3:1, Matthew 28:20, and Matthew 6:14.

GOD KEPT HIS PROMISE. HE GAVE SARAH AND ABRAHAM A SON, DESPITE THEIR AGE.

GOD HAS MADE ME LAUGH. EVERYONE WHO HEARS ABOUT THIS WILL LAUGH WITH ME!

THE BABY BOY WAS NAMED ISAAC, WHICH MEANS "LAUGHTER."

A Test of Faith

Abraham—The Tested

Have you ever waited forever to get something you wanted? Perhaps it was a cool video game, and you had to wait until your birthday to get it. Now imagine that soon after you got it, your parents told you to give that game back. What would you do?

Abraham found himself in this situation, except that it was much harder! He had waited twenty-five years for Isaac—the son God had promised—to be born. Abraham watched Isaac grow up and loved him so much. But one day God asked Abraham to do the impossible: "Take your son to the mountain of Moriah and sacrifice him." Abraham was heartbroken. He could have refused. But he didn't.

God had promised to make Abraham's descendants as numerous as the stars. And Abraham believed God would keep that promise. So the next day he took Isaac up the mountain.

TAKE YOUR SON, YOUR BELOVED ISAAC, AND GO WITH HIM TO MORIAH. THERE YOU MUST SACRIFICE HIM.

WHERE: MOUNT MORIAH, WHERE SOLOMON LATER BUILT THE TEMPLE OF THE LORD

DID YOU KNOW? ABRAHAM WAS KNOWN AS GOD'S FRIEND (2 CHRONICLES 20:7; ISAIAH 41:8).

The sacrifice God wants is a willing spirit.
—PSALM 51:17 ICB

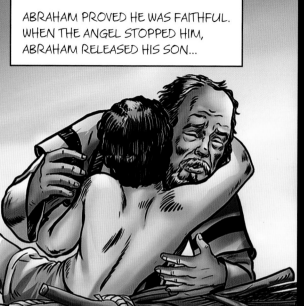

ABRAHAM PROVED HE WAS FAITHFUL. WHEN THE ANGEL STOPPED HIM, ABRAHAM RELEASED HIS SON...

...AND WENT TO FETCH THE RAM FOR THE SACRIFICE INSTEAD.

Just as Abraham raised the knife to sacrifice his son, an angel stopped him. "God knows that you trust Him because you were willing to sacrifice your cherished son," the angel said. Abraham hugged his son tight. Then he found a ram in the bushes and sacrificed the animal to God. God blessed Abraham and Isaac with many more years together.

Abraham was ready to give up the son he loved to honor God. And God did give up His Son for you. What are you ready to give up for God? ▶ GENESIS 22

🏃 BE A HERO!

Sacrifice means giving up something important to you for someone else. What can you give up to help someone? Perhaps it's a Saturday morning to share homemade treats with the police and firemen who sacrifice so much for you. Or you could give up some of your playtime to help your parents make dinner. Make a sacrifice to help someone this week.

🏃 HERO TRAINING When Jesus came, He changed the way sacrifices were made. It was no longer about animals and priests. Instead, sacrifices became about how we live our lives. Read Romans 12:1. How could choosing to please God—instead of the world, your friends, or even yourself—be a "living sacrifice" to God?

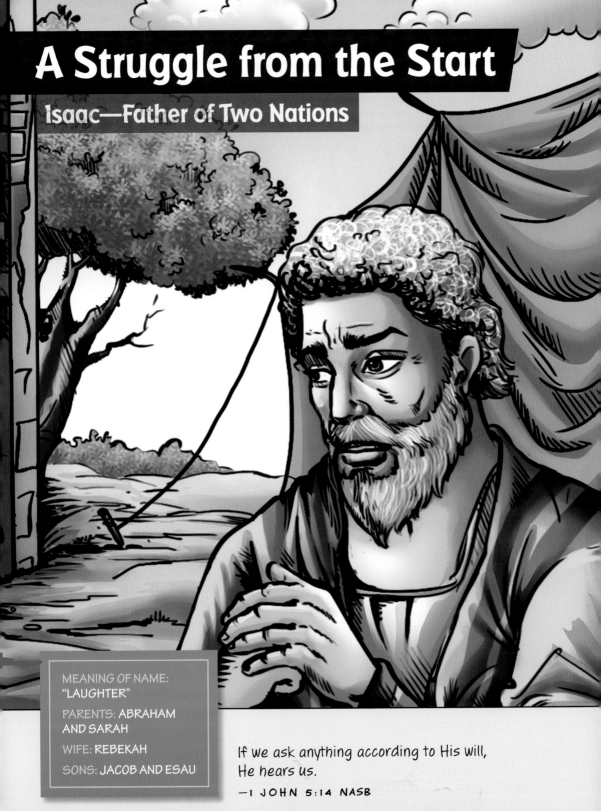

A Struggle from the Start

Isaac—Father of Two Nations

MEANING OF NAME:
"LAUGHTER"

PARENTS: ABRAHAM
AND SARAH

WIFE: REBEKAH

SONS: JACOB AND ESAU

If we ask anything according to His will,
He hears us.

—1 JOHN 5:14 NASB

Do your parents always give you what you ask for? Chances are, they don't. Sometimes it's because you ask for things that aren't good for you—like staying up late to play video games. But other times it's because they have a better plan. For example, your parents may say no to pizza for dinner because they're planning a trip to your favorite restaurant.

God is like that when He answers prayers. He always listens, and He always answers. But God also answers according to His plan.

🦸 BE A HERO!

Great things can happen when we pray for each other. (Read James 5:16 to see for yourself.) Who needs your prayers today? A family member, a friend, someone in your neighborhood or church? The strongest heroes lift others up in prayer.

When Isaac asked God for a child, God answered. But it wasn't in the way Isaac expected. Rebekah did become pregnant—but with twins!

While they were still in Rebekah's womb, the twins struggled against each other. Rebekah asked God why, and He answered her. God said, "Two nations, two separate peoples, will come from you. One will be stronger than the other, and the older will serve the younger."

Those twins fought right up until the moment they were born. And they didn't stop then either! But God had a perfect plan for those twins. One of them—Jacob—would be the father of a new nation, a nation of God's people.

God answered Isaac's prayers, and He answered Rebekah's too. But God doesn't just give you whatever you want. He answers your prayers according to His perfect plan. That plan is to bless you and do good for you—and the whole world too (Jeremiah 29:11). ▶ GENESIS 25

ESAU WAS THE FIRSTBORN. JACOB WAS SECOND.

🏃 HERO TRAINING
In Matthew 6:9–13, Jesus teaches us how to pray. Check out these verses and pay special attention to verse 10. Whose will should be done? Whatever you pray for, ask for God's will to be done. That's always the best plan.

Meeting God

Jacob—The Traveler

Come near to God, and God will come near to you.

—JAMES 4:8 ICB

FATHER: ISAAC

GRANDFATHER: ABRAHAM

KEY TERM: BIRTHRIGHT:
THE INHERITANCE OF THE
FIRSTBORN SON

Have you ever seen your teacher in the grocery store or your pastor at the dentist? Meeting someone you know in an unexpected place can be quite a surprise. Now imagine meeting God on the way to your uncle's house. That's what happened to Jacob!

Jacob was running away from the trouble he'd created. First, he had traded with his older brother, Esau, giving a bowl of stew for the birthright of the firstborn son. Then Jacob had tricked their father, Isaac, into giving him the blessings that were normally given to the firstborn son. By now, Esau wanted to kill Jacob. So their mother, Rebekah, urged Jacob to run away to his uncle's house.

It was a long journey, and Jacob stopped to rest for the night. As he slept, he dreamed of a stairway to heaven. It was filled with angels walking up and down. God spoke to Jacob, saying, "I am the God of Abraham and Isaac. I will give you this land. And your descendants will be as many as the dust of the earth." God also promised to go with Jacob. God would protect Jacob wherever he went. When Jacob awoke, he knew he had just met with God.

God also promises to go with you and protect you wherever you go (Psalm 121:5–8). Whether it's across the lunchroom to sit with someone who always sits alone or across your neighborhood with your parents to welcome someone new to your town, God will be with you!

▶ GENESIS 27–28

🏃 **HERO TRAINING** Jacob never expected to hear God's voice that night. But you can expect to hear God's voice every day. Just be still and listen. He might whisper a verse into your heart. He might send someone to encourage you. And He always speaks through the Bible. God loves to talk to you!

🏃 **BE A HERO!**

Heroes are kind to everyone they meet. Make it a habit to treat everyone, from the waitress to the president, as if he or she were God's angel. After all, Hebrews 13:1–2 says you never know who you might meet!

15

Wrestling with God

Jacob—A New Name

MEANING OF NAME: "DECEITFUL" OR "ONE WHO TAKES THE HEEL"

ALSO KNOWN AS: ISRAEL, MEANING "PRINCE WITH GOD" OR "WRESTLED WITH GOD"; ISRAEL LATER BECAME THE NAME OF THE ENTIRE JEWISH NATION

WIVES: LEAH AND RACHEL

See what great love the Father has lavished on us, that we should be called children of God! And that is what we are!

—1 JOHN 3:1 NIV

Think about your name for a minute. Is it a family name? Were you named after a parent, grandparent, or special uncle or aunt? Or perhaps yours is a special name your parents picked out just for you.

In Bible times, names weren't just what you were called. They also said something about who you were. So when God changed someone's name, He was also changing who that person would be.

Jacob experienced such a change. Years had passed since Jacob had fled his brother Esau's anger. Now he was returning home with his wives and children to make peace. One night Jacob waited alone near the river and prepared to meet Esau. Suddenly, a stranger appeared and began to wrestle with Jacob. They fought for hours, but Jacob wouldn't give up!

As morning approached, the stranger struck Jacob's hip, injuring him. Still, Jacob wouldn't let go! "What is your name?" the stranger asked. When Jacob answered, the stranger said, "Your name is now Israel because you have wrestled with God and man—and won!"

Jacob knew he had seen God face-to-face. As the sun rose that morning, Jacob was no longer "the deceitful." He was Israel, the one who "wrestled with God."

When you decide to follow God, He gives you a new name too—child of God!
▶ GENESIS 32

I HAVE SEEN THE **FACE OF GOD,** AND I AM STILL ALIVE!

🏃 **HERO TRAINING** Part of growing up is figuring out who you are. The world will tell you all sorts of things—things that aren't true. Always turn to God to find out who you really are. Start with these beautiful verses: 1 John 3:1, Galatians 4:7, Psalm 139:13–14, and 1 Peter 2:9.

🦸 BE A HERO!

Do you ever "wrestle" with getting along with someone? Perhaps it's a brother or sister, a neighbor, or someone at school. When someone around you is being difficult, try adding this phrase to their name: "loved by God." Because heroes remember that everyone is loved by God.

Letting Go

Jacob and Esau—Brothers Again

Have you ever been so angry with others that you couldn't stand to look at them? Or maybe you hurt someone's feelings so badly that you were afraid of what he or she might say back to you. That's what happened between Jacob and Esau.

PARENTS: ISAAC AND REBEKAH

WHEN: 20 YEARS AFTER JACOB RAN FROM ESAU

"When you offer your gift to God at the altar, and you remember that your brother has something against you, leave your gift there at the altar. Go and make peace with him. Then come and offer your gift."

—MATTHEW 5:23-24 ICB

Jacob and Esau were twins, but they were nothing alike. They didn't look alike or think alike. There was trouble between them right from the start; they even fought before they were born!

Twenty years after Jacob tricked Esau out of his birthright and stole the blessing that should have been given to Esau, God told Jacob to return home. But would Esau forgive Jacob?

To soften his brother's heart, Jacob sent gifts ahead. Then he saw Esau riding out to meet him with four hundred of his men. Jacob was truly frightened!

But as the brothers came face-to-face for the first time in so many years, a wonderful thing happened—Esau ran to hug Jacob. All was forgiven, and they were brothers again.

Esau had plenty of reasons to be angry. But he let go of that anger and forgave his brother. It's not an easy thing to do, but when you're angry, God wants you to let go and forgive too. ▶ *GENESIS 31–33*

🏃 HERO TRAINING Part of forgiving is keeping your focus off the thing that made you hurt or angry. It's leaving what happened in the past, in the past. Look at Philippians 3:12–14. Instead of focusing on the past, what should you think about?

🦸 BE A HERO!

Jacob knew he had cheated his brother. Though it took several years, he was eventually willing to go back and make peace. When you mess up, don't wait to make it right. Say you're sorry and try to solve the problem. Heroes make peace with others.

JACOB FINALLY MET HIS BROTHER.

I AM SO HAPPY TO SEE YOU!

ACCEPT THE GIFTS I HAVE SENT TO YOU.

I SHALL, MY BROTHER.

JACOB AND ESAU WEPT AS THEY WERE REUNITED AS BROTHERS AGAIN.

When Jealousy Strikes

Joseph—The Slave

Peace of mind means a healthy body. But jealousy will rot your bones.

—PROVERBS 14:30 ICB

WHERE: CANAAN

AGE: JOSEPH WAS ABOUT 17 YEARS OLD WHEN HE BECAME A SLAVE

What if you lost everything in one moment? What if your whole world changed because someone was jealous of what you had? That's exactly what happened to Joseph.

Joseph was Jacob's favorite son. Jacob even gave him a special coat to prove it. This did not make Joseph's brothers happy. In fact, they were so jealous that they hated Joseph. And when Joseph told his brothers how they all bowed down to him in his dreams, well, let's just say that didn't help.

One day, as Joseph's brothers were tending sheep, they saw him coming. "Here comes that dreamer," one said. "Let's kill him!" But another said, "No. Let's throw him in this pit." So they grabbed him, ripped off his coat, and tossed him into the pit.

When the brothers saw a band of traders approaching, they got an idea: "Let's sell Joseph!" They hauled their brother up out of the pit and sold him as a slave. Joseph lost his home, his family, everything—all because of his brothers' jealousy.

When someone else has what you want, jealousy can easily creep in. Fight jealousy by lifting that person up in your prayers. After all, it's hard to have hard feelings about someone you're praying for! ▶ *GENESIS 37*

⚑ BE A HERO!

Stamp out jealousy before it starts. Instead of thinking about what you don't have, think of all you do have. But don't stop there—think of all you can share. Because a grateful and giving heart stops jealousy in its tracks! What can you share today?

🏃 **HERO TRAINING** Jealousy is wanting for yourself what belongs to someone else. And it's so serious that God listed it in the Ten Commandments as one of the things we must not do. Read Exodus 20:17 for yourself. Why do you think God is serious about jealousy? What problems does it cause?

JOSEPH WALKED TOWARD EGYPT WITH HIS CAPTORS, NOT KNOWING HIS FATE.

When the Time Was Right

Joseph—Who Waited for God

> EVEN AS HE WAS LOCKED IN PRISON, THE LORD WAS WITH JOSEPH.

Life is full of all kinds of experiences—from amazing, top-of-the-world experiences to down-in-a-deep-dark-pit experiences. Joseph knew all about both.

You see, Joseph went from favorite son to slave in just one day. But even as a slave in Egypt, Joseph managed to find success. Because God was with him.

When Joseph was thrown into prison for something he didn't do, Joseph stayed true to God. Later, when God helped him explain a dream for Pharaoh's cupbearer, Joseph began to hope for a way out of prison. But the cupbearer forgot all about Joseph.

Then, two years later, Pharaoh had a troubling dream. Finally, the cupbearer

AGE: SOLD INTO SLAVERY AT 17 YEARS OLD; RELEASED FROM PRISON AT 30 YEARS OLD

JOBS: SHEPHERD, SLAVE, AND RULER OF EGYPT

Wait for the Lord's help. Be strong and brave and wait for the Lord's help.
—PSALM 27:14 ICB

remembered Joseph. One moment, Joseph was in prison. The next, he was standing before Pharaoh! With God's help, Joseph explained Pharaoh's dream. Pharaoh was so impressed that he made Joseph second in command over Egypt.

For thirteen years, Joseph had been either a slave or a prisoner. He could've tried to run away, escape, or fix things himself. But he didn't. Joseph trusted God. He waited for God to rescue him. And when the time was right, that's exactly what God did.

Like Joseph, you'll have some tough days. But don't try to fix everything on your own. Talk to God, trust that He is with you, and honor Him as you wait for His perfect plan.

▶ *Genesis 40–41*

🏃 HERO TRAINING You just know you're ready to stay home alone or old enough to bike to the neighborhood store with friends. But Mom and Dad say you're not quite old enough. While you wait, memorize Luke 16:10. Then show them how responsible you can be. Fix your own snacks. Put your bike away. Take care of little things, and your parents will trust you to do bigger things when the time is right.

🏃 BE A HERO!

Waiting isn't very fun. Even waiting in line can be annoying sometimes. But you can make it easier—even fun! If you're with friends or siblings, take turns telling silly stories. Whoever makes the others laugh wins!

Everything for Good

Joseph—The Forgiver

PHARAOH GAVE JOSEPH THE JOB OF PREPARING ALL OF EGYPT FOR THE FAMINE HE HAD PREDICTED. HE BECAME MORE POWERFUL THAN ANY MAN IN EGYPT OTHER THAN PHARAOH.

WIFE: ASENATH

SONS: MANASSEH AND EPHRAIM

AGE: JOSEPH WAS ABOUT 39 YEARS OLD WHEN HIS BROTHERS FIRST CAME TO EGYPT

LIFE SPAN: DIED AT AGE 110

We know that in everything God works for the good of those who love him.

—ROMANS 8:28 ICB

Have you ever needed to forgive someone? Was it easy to do? Or did you struggle with wanting revenge instead?

Joseph faced that same choice. Though his brothers had sold him into slavery, he was now second in command of Egypt. God had warned Joseph that a famine was coming, so he collected and stored grain to get ready. When the famine came, the people of Egypt had food. But outside of Egypt, the people were starving—including Joseph's family.

🕴 BE A HERO!

God can bring good out of every bad thing. And He can use you to do it. Ask God how you can be part of His plans for good. Perhaps you can visit an older person who lives alone. Or maybe you can help a younger child who's struggling to read.

Joseph's brothers traveled to Egypt and stood before Joseph to buy food. Joseph had a choice to make: he could forgive them, or he could get revenge. After all, he was a powerful man. He could have let his brothers starve, sold them as slaves, or thrown them into prison.

Joseph chose to forgive. "You meant to hurt me," he told his brothers. "But God turned your evil into good and saved the lives of many people."

Forgiving others doesn't mean it was okay that they hurt you. It does mean that you trust God to bring good out of the bad. When someone hurts you, remember Joseph. Choose to forgive. ▶*GENESIS 41–45, 50*

🏃 **HERO TRAINING** Those who crucified Jesus intended great harm, but God used their evil to bring about the greatest good of all. Look up 1 Peter 3:18, Hebrews 4:14–16, and John 14:2–3. What good things did God bring out of their evil plans?

Behind the Scenes

Jochebed—The Courageous

Have you ever been backstage at a play? While a lot is happening onstage, there's even more going on backstage. The workers behind the scenes lower backdrops, move sets, and shine lights on the actors. God is often like those people. We may not see Him, but He's always working to keep everything moving in the right direction.

MAY THE LORD PROTECT YOU, MY SON.

TO SAVE HER SON'S LIFE, THE MOTHER PLACED HER CHILD IN A BASKET MADE OF BULRUSHES AND PUT IT IN THE RIVER.

HUSBAND: AMRAM

CHILDREN: AARON, MIRIAM, AND MOSES

JOB: AN ISRAELITE SLAVE IN EGYPT

Jesus said to them, "My Father never stops working."
—JOHN 5:17 ICB

Consider the story of Jochebed and her baby boy. Nearly four hundred years had passed since the days of Joseph. The new pharaoh of Egypt did not know who Joseph was or how he had saved the Egyptians from famine. And he didn't like how many Israelites there were. He thought they might become stronger than the Egyptians. So he made them all slaves. Even worse, the pharaoh ordered that every newborn Israelite boy be thrown into the Nile River!

For three months, Jochebed hid her beautiful son. When he grew too big to keep hidden, she carefully put him in a basket. Then—bravely trusting God—she placed the basket in the reeds near the river. Her daughter, Miriam, watched and waited nearby.

Pharaoh's own daughter found the baby and felt sorry for him. At that moment, Miriam rushed up and offered to find a woman to take care of the baby. And who did Miriam run to get? Jochebed! That baby was Moses, and when he grew up, he led God's people out of slavery.

None of this happened by accident. God was working the whole time behind the scenes. And that's exactly what He does in your life too. ▶ EXODUS 1–2

🏃 HERO TRAINING
It took great courage for Jochebed to put her baby in that basket. Even when you know God is working in your life, it takes courage to trust Him. Read Psalm 3:3. How is God like a shield? How does He give you courage?

🦸 BE A HERO!

Matthew 6:1 encourages us to do good things in secret. How can you secretly help today? Can you sneakily take out the trash? Maybe you can rake the leaves from your older neighbor's yard. Or drop an encouraging note at someone's front door. Be a hero who helps behind the scenes.

Fire!

Moses—A Nervous Shepherd

Have you ever been asked to do a job you didn't think you could do? Maybe it was organizing a group project or reading a story out loud in class. Whatever it was, you weren't sure you were the right person for the job!

Moses would completely understand that feeling. You see, after Pharaoh's daughter rescued him, Moses grew up as a prince in Egypt. But then he committed a terrible crime. Moses ran away from Pharaoh's anger and became a shepherd in a nearby country.

MOSES ENCOUNTERED A BUSH THAT WAS ON FIRE, YET IT WOULDN'T BURN.

WHY DOESN'T THE FIRE CONSUME THIS BUSH?

GOD THEN CALLED OUT TO MOSES, THE LORD'S VOICE COMING FROM THE BURNING BUSH.

MOSES!

I AM HERE!

PARENTS: AMRAM AND JOCHEBED

SIBLINGS: AARON AND MIRIAM

WIFE: ZIPPORAH

SONS: GERSHOM AND ELIEZER

The God of peace will give you every good thing you need so that you can do what he wants.
—HEBREWS 13:20 ICB

One day, as he was out with his flocks, Moses saw the strangest thing. A bush was on fire, yet it didn't burn up! When Moses went to take a closer look, God called to him from the bush: "Go to Pharaoh. Tell him to set My people free!"

Moses wasn't so sure he was the right person for that job. He offered God excuse after excuse. But God promised to be with him. God gave Moses special signs to perform. He even agreed to send Moses' brother, Aaron, to do the talking. God gave Moses everything he needed to do the job.

BE A HERO!

Hebrews 13:20–21 tells us God will give us whatever we need to follow Him. Sometimes that means He'll send other people to help us, just as He sent Aaron to help Moses. So don't be afraid to ask for—and accept—help. Heroes not only help others; they let others help them too.

One day God will give you a job you don't think you can do. It might be standing up for someone being bullied or moving to a new place or writing a book about God. Just remember Moses. And know God will give you everything you need to obey Him. ▶ *Exodus 2–4*

✗ HERO TRAINING Check out Exodus 4:1–9. What signs did God give Moses? These signs were to help Moses prove to the Israelites that God had sent him. Do you think those signs helped Moses believe too?

Lord Over All

Moses—The Messenger

Have you ever watched a storm roll in? Did you notice the roar of the wind, the pounding rain, and the power of the lightning? Storms give us just a tiny glimpse of the power of God.

The power of thunderstorms is nothing compared to the power of the plagues God unleashed on Egypt. You see, Moses did take God's message to Egypt's ruler, but Pharaoh

WHEN MOSES ASKED PHARAOH TO LET HIS PEOPLE GO, PHARAOH REFUSED, AND THE **NILE RIVER TURNED TO BLOOD**. PEOPLE RAN FROM ITS BANKS BECAUSE OF ITS SICK SMELL. THOUSANDS OF FISH WASHED UP ON THE SHORE—**DEAD!**

AGE: *80 YEARS OLD* WHEN HE SPOKE TO PHARAOH

TRIBE: LEVI

KNOWN FOR: THE SAYING "LET MY PEOPLE GO!"

No one is like you, LORD; you are great, and your name is mighty in power.
—JEREMIAH 10:6 NIV

refused to listen. After all, he was the most powerful man in Egypt. Why should he obey a God he didn't know?

That's when God began sending plagues to prove that He—and only He—was Lord over all. First, all the water turned to blood. Then frogs, gnats, and flies invaded the land. Livestock died, boils covered both people and animals, and hail rained from the sky. Next came locusts and darkness. Yet Pharaoh still wouldn't let the Israelites go free. Then came the most terrible plague of all: the plague of death. Only then did Pharaoh say to Moses, "Get out! You and your people leave Egypt at once!" Not even Pharaoh could stand against the power of God.

As you grow up, you'll meet people who refuse to believe God has any power. Just watch that next storm roll in, remember Pharaoh, and know that your God is the most powerful of all!

▶ *Exodus 4–12*

AFTER THE FINAL PLAGUE, PHARAOH KNEW HE HAD BEEN BEATEN. HIS POWER WAS NOT GREATER THAN THE GOD OF MOSES.

🏋 HERO TRAINING

Psalm 19:1 says that "the heavens declare the glory of God" (NIV). Check out these verses to see other ways God has shown His power through nature: Genesis 1, Mark 4:35–41, and Joshua 10:12–14.

🏃 BE A HERO!

No trouble you face or battle you fight is bigger than God. Sometimes, though, that's hard to remember. When you need help or someone you know is struggling, shout out your faith for all the world to hear: *God is bigger!* Because there's no hero more powerful than God.

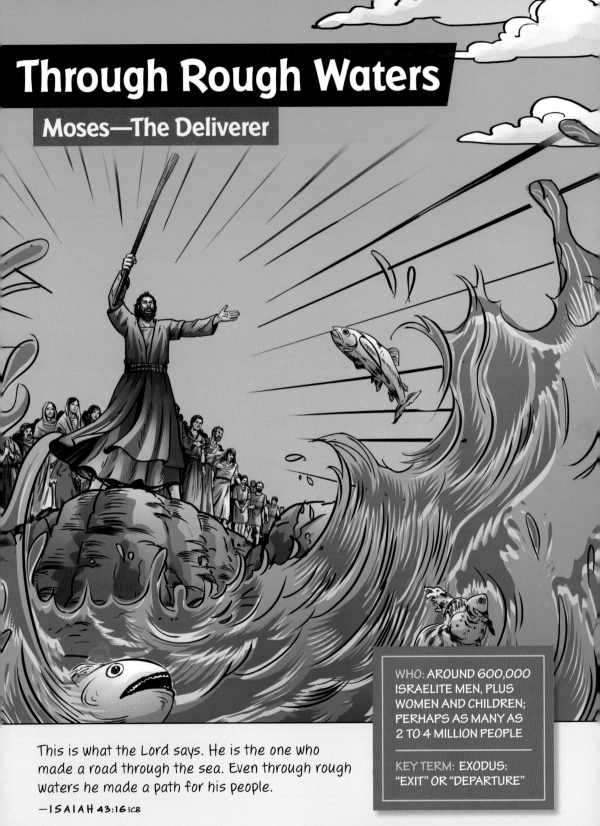

Through Rough Waters

Moses—The Deliverer

This is what the Lord says. He is the one who made a road through the sea. Even through rough waters he made a path for his people.

—ISAIAH 43:16 ICB

WHO: AROUND 600,000 ISRAELITE MEN, PLUS WOMEN AND CHILDREN; PERHAPS AS MANY AS 2 TO 4 MILLION PEOPLE

KEY TERM: EXODUS: "EXIT" OR "DEPARTURE"

imagine you're walking through the mall with your family. You stop to look at a cool toy in a store's window. When you turn back, your family isn't there! Now a big line of people is blocking your way. You feel trapped, and you don't know what to do!

The Israelites knew what it was like to feel trapped. Moses had led them out of Egypt, but Pharaoh decided he didn't want the Israelites to leave after all. So a big group of Egyptian soldiers chased after them. The Israelites were terrified. In front of them, the rough waters of the Red Sea splashed. Behind, the Egyptians were getting closer by the minute!

The Israelites didn't know how things would be okay. But God had a plan to save them. God told Moses to lift his walking stick over the Red Sea. Moses obeyed, and the rough waters split apart! The Israelites walked across the sea on dry land. They were safe.

When you feel trapped and aren't sure what to do, ask God for help. He'll get you through the rough waters and will guide you to safety. ▶ *Exodus 14*

 BE A HERO!

How can you lead someone to safety? Maybe you can help a younger student at school find his classroom. Or you could teach your younger sister to look both ways before crossing the street. Share your ideas with your family, and make a plan to lead someone to safety this week!

🏃 HERO TRAINING Did you know that hard times can be good for you? Challenges build your faith muscles because they teach you to rely on God. Memorize James 1:2–4. The next time you face something difficult, say these verses out loud. And trust that God will take care of you!

Bread of Heaven

Moses—Who Trusted God

Your body needs all kinds of things to stay healthy, like air to breathe, clothing to wear, and shelter from harsh weather. But nothing is more important to your health than food and water. You can survive for only about three weeks without food. You'll live only about three days without water.

IN THE MORNING, THE PEOPLE FOUND A GIFT FROM THE LORD—THE GROUND WAS COVERED WITH MANNA, A SPECIAL BREAD THEY COULD EAT.

GOD TOLD MOSES TO STRIKE A ROCK AT HOREB (SINAI) WITH HIS STAFF, AND WATER FLOWED FROM IT.

MOSES DID AS GOD COMMANDED, AND WHEN THE REST OF THE HEBREWS ARRIVED, THEY HAD PLENTY OF WATER TO DRINK.

KNOWN FOR: BEING THE MOST HUMBLE MAN ON EARTH

KEY TERM: MANNA: LITERAL MEANING: "WHAT IS IT?"; MYSTERIOUS FLAKES OF FOOD THAT GOD SENT EACH MORNING THE ISRAELITES LIVED IN THE WILDERNESS; ALSO CALLED "BREAD OF ANGELS" IN PSALM 78

My God will supply all your needs according to His riches in glory in Christ Jesus.
—PHILIPPIANS 4:19 NASB

So you can imagine why the Israelites were a bit worried and grumbly. They had been traveling in the desert for three days without finding a drop of water to drink or a bite of food to eat. Yes, they had just miraculously escaped Pharaoh by walking through the Red Sea, but now they were tired, thirsty, and hungry.

The Israelites complained to Moses. Moses cried out to God. And God? Well, He gave them water from a rock. And He sent flocks of quail for them to eat. But perhaps most amazing of all, He sent manna. This mysterious bread from heaven covered the ground each morning like a flaky dew. The Israelites gathered what they needed, and it was always just enough.

Even though the Israelites struggled to trust God, He was always faithful to provide what they needed. And He'll always provide what you truly need too. Don't be like those grumbling Israelites. Trust God to take care of you.

▶ EXODUS 15–17

✗ BE A HERO!

God often uses people to provide what we need—people like you. Take a look around. What needs do you see? Maybe it's something small like clothes in your room that need to be put away. Or perhaps it's something bigger, like collecting warm mittens for foster kids. Heroes let God use them to meet others' needs.

✗ HERO TRAINING

Moses spoke to God for the people. But because Jesus came, you don't need anyone to talk to God for you. You can talk to Him yourself! Ask Him for what you need. And trust Him to take care of you, just as He promises in Philippians 4:19.

MOSES PROMISED THE ISRAELITES THEY WOULD HAVE MEAT. THEN GOD SENT QUAIL TO THEIR CAMP.

The Commandments of God

Moses—Who Talked with God

THE ISRAELITES ARRIVED AT MOUNT SINAI—THE SAME PLACE WHERE MOSES HAD FIRST ENCOUNTERED GOD.

Rules! Rules! Rules! They're everywhere, and sometimes it seems that they're just stopping you from doing what you want. But the truth is, most rules are made to keep you safe. For example, the rule to not dive into a shallow pool keeps you from hitting your head.

In the wilderness, God gave the Israelites rules. But the rules weren't to stop the people

MOSES VENTURED ALONE UP THE MOUNTAIN PATH TO TALK TO GOD.

LIFE SPAN: 120 YEARS OLD

WRITER: MOSES WROTE GENESIS, EXODUS, LEVITICUS, NUMBERS, AND MOST OF DEUTERONOMY

BURIAL SITE: UNKNOWN; GOD HIMSELF BURIED MOSES SOMEWHERE IN MOAB

DID YOU KNOW? MOSES SPOKE WITH GOD FACE-TO-FACE (EXODUS 33:11).

The Lord's teachings are perfect. They give new strength. . . . The Lord's commands are pure. They light up the way.

—PSALM 19:7-8 ICB

from having fun. They were to keep them safe and help them be holy.

The Israelites had been traveling for about three months. They had left Egypt, but some of the Egyptians' bad habits had not left them—habits like worshipping phony gods. That's why God called Moses up to the top of Mount Sinai.

On the mountain, God spoke to Moses. He told Moses how His people should live and how they should love Him. With His own finger, God wrote the Ten Commandments on two tablets of stone. The first four commandments told the people how to love and honor God. The last six told them how to love and respect each other. God promised that if the Israelites would keep His commandments, then He would make them His people.

God's commandments, or rules, weren't made to take anything away from the people. They were made to give them—and you—a blessed and holy life. When you're tempted to break a rule, stop and think. How might that rule be keeping you safe or helping you honor God? ▶ *EXODUS 19–20, 31*

LATER MOSES DESCENDED THE MOUNTAIN CARRYING GOD'S COMMANDMENTS ETCHED IN TWO STONE TABLETS.

🏃 **HERO TRAINING** The Ten Comandments aren't the only laws in the Old Testament. There are about six hundred others! Jesus summed them up in just two commandments. You can find them in Matthew 22:34–40. How different would the world be if everyone followed these two commandments?

🦸 BE A HERO!

Imagine playing a game without any rules. It would be a mess! To help you remember why rules are important, volunteer to teach some younger kids a new game. Be sure to carefully explain all the rules. After all, heroes understand that rules help keep everyone safe and happy.

Into the Promised Land

Joshua—The Chosen Leader

Show me the right path, O LORD; point out the road for me to follow. Lead me by your truth and teach me, for you are the God who saves me.

—PSALM 25:4–5 NLT

BIRTHPLACE: EGYPT

FATHER: NUN, OF THE TRIBE OF EPHRAIM

KNOWN FOR: BEING A LEADER AND MIGHTY WARRIOR FOR GOD

Have you ever played follow-the-leader with a lousy leader? Maybe someone led you down a steep, rocky path, and you knew you shouldn't go down it. If so, then you know how important it is to have a good leader—someone who will keep you safe and help you find the right way to go.

The Israelites had been following Moses through the wilderness for forty years. He was a good leader, but he had grown old. His time on earth was ending. God told Moses to choose Joshua as Israel's new leader. Moses called Joshua to him and said, "You will lead this people into the promised land. Be strong. Be brave. Because the Lord Himself will be with you. He will not leave you or forget you. So don't be afraid, and don't worry."

Moses then climbed up on Mount Nebo. There, God allowed him to see the promised land. Moses died on the mountain, and God buried him.

With Moses gone, Joshua became Israel's leader. He marched the Israelites to the edge of the Jordan River. It was time to take the promised land.

Moses had been a good leader because he followed God. God chose Joshua to lead because Joshua followed Him too. One day you'll have the chance to be a leader. Make sure you are ready then by following God now. ▶ *DEUTERONOMY 31–34; JOSHUA 1*

HERO TRAINING The world likes leaders who are tough and strong and proud. But Jesus has a different definition of leadership. Look up Mark 10:42–45. Do Jesus' words change the way you want to lead others?

WITH MOSES GONE, JOSHUA TOOK CHARGE. HE MARCHED THE HEBREWS TO THE BORDER OF THE PROMISED LAND.

Saved!

Rahab—The Believer

WHERE: RAHAB'S HOUSE, BUILT INTO THE WALLS OF JERICHO

DID YOU KNOW? RAHAB IS ONE OF ONLY FIVE WOMEN NAMED IN THE FAMILY HISTORY OF JESUS (MATTHEW 1:1–17).

It was by faith that Rahab . . . welcomed the spies and was not killed with those who refused to obey God.

—HEBREWS 11:31 ICB

What you believe determines what you do. For example, if you believe school is over when the bell rings, you'll get up to leave when you hear the bell. If you believe you'll fall off your bike if you don't hold on, you'll hold on.

Rahab believed something no one else in her city believed. Her belief made her willing to do something no one else would do. You see, Rahab lived in Jericho, but she had heard about the Israelites and their God and the battles they had already won. And she was frightened!

When Joshua's two spies came to Jericho, Rahab hid them on the roof of her house. The king's men came looking for the spies, but Rahab lied to protect them—risking her own life.

Later, she told the spies how the whole city was terrified of the Israelites. "Because," she said, "the Lord your God rules the heavens above and the earth below!"

Rahab was not an Israelite. And her own people looked down on her. But Rahab believed that God was Lord of all. She had faith. And because she was willing to act on that faith, she and her whole family were safe when Jericho fell.

Do you have faith like Rahab did? Do you believe that "the Lord your God rules the heavens above and the earth below"? What are you willing to do about it? ▸JOSHUA 2

BE A HERO!

Rahab wasn't an Israelite. She wasn't respected in her community. But she was loved by God and chosen to be part of Jesus' family tree—a huge honor! You will meet some unpopular people, like Rahab, but remember that they need love too. Heroes know that everyone matters to God. So treat everyone you meet with love and kindness.

🏃 **HERO TRAINING** Rahab was saved because she believed God was Lord over all—not because of anything she did. Look up Ephesians 2:8. How are you saved? Remember, there's nothing you can do that will make God love you more or less.

Crumbling, Tumbling Down

Joshua—The Obedient

GOD SENT AN ANGEL TO TELL JOSHUA HIS PLAN TO WIN THE BATTLE OF JERICHO.

WE MUST MARCH AROUND THE CITY WALL!

Some people think that to win, they must do things their own way. But Joshua, one of Israel's greatest warriors, knew that victory didn't come from himself or his strength. It came from obeying God, the One with real power and strength. Joshua obeyed God, even when what God asked him to do just didn't make sense.

One of Joshua's very first challenges as Israel's leader was the Battle of Jericho. He knew it would be a tough battle. The

JOSHUA AND THE ISRAELITES MARCHED TO THE OUT-SKIRTS OF JERICHO. THEY FOLLOWED GOD'S PLAN AND MARCHED AROUND THE CITY EACH DAY FOR A WEEK.

MEANING OF NAME: "GOD SAVES"; *JOSHUA* IS THE HEBREW FORM OF *JESUS*

DEATH: IN CANAAN, THE PROMISED LAND, AT 110 YEARS OLD

Don't just listen to God's word. You must do what it says.

—JAMES 1:22 NLT

city was surrounded by towering walls, and the chances of Joshua and his men knocking down those walls on their own were pretty much zero.

But Joshua wasn't on his own. God sent an angel, the commander of His heavenly armies, to tell Joshua exactly how to win. God's plan, though, was unlike any battle plan Joshua had ever heard. *March around the city? Blow trumpets? Shout?* It didn't make sense.

Joshua trusted the Lord anyway. For seven days, the Israelites marched around the walls of Jericho. After seven laps on the seventh day, they blew the trumpets and shouted—and Jericho's massive walls tumbled down.

🦸 BE A HERO!

God gave Joshua unexpected directions to defeat Israel's enemy. He has also given us directions about how to fight our enemies, and they are just as surprising! Jesus said to pray for our enemies. Next time you're mad at someone, try praying for him or her. You might be surprised at how God answers.

Imagine how different that story would be if Joshua had decided to do things his own way. Those walls would have stayed right where they were. The next time you're tempted to do things your own way, remember Joshua and those tumbling walls and follow God's directions.

▸*Joshua 5–6*

🦸 **HERO TRAINING** Read John 14:23. When you choose to obey Jesus' teachings, what does that say about how you feel about Him? And what promise does He give you?

ON THE SEVENTH DAY THE PRIESTS BLEW THEIR TRUMPETS LOUDLY. THEN ON JOSHUA'S COMMAND, ALL THE ISRAELITES SHOUTED AT THE TOP OF THEIR VOICES. SUDDENLY, THE WALLS OF THE GREAT CITY TUMBLED TO THE GROUND IN A CLOUD OF DUST AND ROCK.

SHOUT! FOR THE LORD HAS GIVEN YOU THE CITY.

THE ISRAELITES DREW THEIR SWORDS AND GRABBED THEIR SPEARS. THE CITY WAS NOW OPEN.

Leading the Charge!
Deborah—The Bold

Have you ever watched a roller coaster whiz by and wished you had the courage to give it a try? What would have happened if a friend grabbed your hand and said, "Let's go!" Sometimes it takes one person being brave and bold to encourage others to do the same.

Deborah was that bold person. For twenty years, the Canaanites had ruled over Israel and treated the Israelites horribly. When the Israelites cried out to God, He used Deborah to help.

Deborah was both a prophet and Israel's judge. One day God gave Deborah a message for Barak, the commander of Israel's army: "The Lord commands you to attack Sisera and his army. God will give him into your hands."

Sisera was the leader of the Canaanite army, and

MEANING OF NAME: "BEE"

JOBS: PROPHET AND FOURTH JUDGE OF ISRAEL

WRITER: DEBORAH WROTE THE "SONG OF DEBORAH," FOUND IN JUDGES 5, CELEBRATING THE LORD'S VICTORY OVER THE CANAANITES

Villagers in Israel would not fight; they held back until I, Deborah, arose, until I arose, a mother in Israel.

—JUDGES 5:7 NIV

Barak wasn't so sure about attacking him. Sisera's army had nine hundred iron chariots! "I won't go unless you go with me," he told Deborah. So Deborah went. And God helped the Israelites destroy Sisera's army. All because one woman was bold enough to trust that God would do what He promised.

God sometimes asks you to do things that require bravery and boldness. Sometimes you need a person who is willing to lead the way. And sometimes you need to be that brave and bold person. ▶*JUDGES 4–5*

BE A HERO!

Someone has to go first. Someone has to be brave first. Let it be you. Walk across the lunchroom to meet the new kid. Take a plate of cookies to that grumpy neighbor and tell her what you learned about God this week. Volunteer to lead the prayer. Go ahead. Be brave. Be bold. Be a hero!

HERO TRAINING God won't ever ask you to be brave all alone. Just look at the promise of Joshua 1:9. And then check out Philippians 4:13. God will give you the strength to do whatever He asks you to do. Yes, being brave can be scary, but who always wins in the end? Find the answer in John 16:33.

Mighty for God

Gideon—God's Soldier

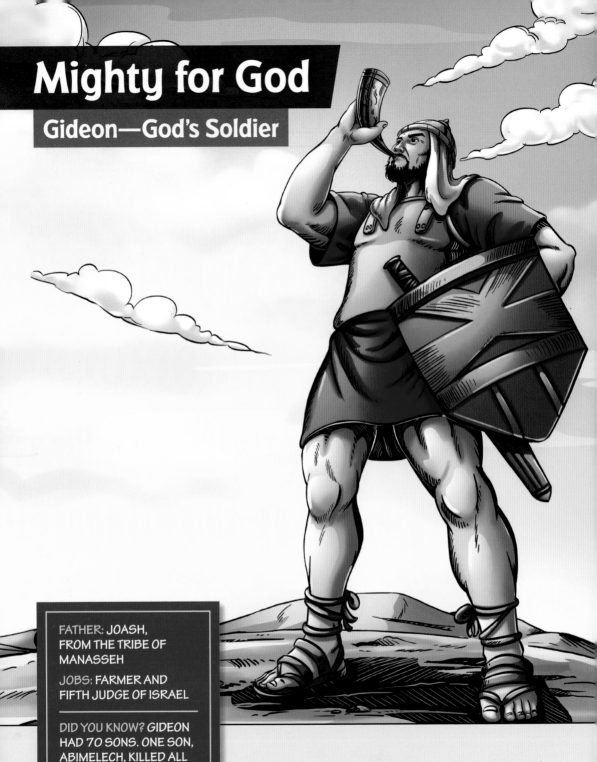

FATHER: JOASH, FROM THE TRIBE OF MANASSEH

JOBS: FARMER AND FIFTH JUDGE OF ISRAEL

DID YOU KNOW? GIDEON HAD 70 SONS. ONE SON, ABIMELECH, KILLED ALL THE OTHER SONS EXCEPT THE YOUNGEST, JOTHAM.

God is working in you, giving you the desire and the power to do what pleases him.
—PHILIPPIANS 2:13 NLT

Have you ever tried to be invisible? Maybe it was in school. You didn't know the answer, so you tried to slink down in your desk to avoid catching the teacher's eye. Or perhaps you forgot to finish a chore, so you tried to sneak past your mom and into your room.

Gideon would completely understand. As the least important person in his family, from the weakest tribe in all Israel, he probably felt invisible sometimes. And when an angel appeared to him, he was hiding and actually trying to be invisible. Imagine Gideon's surprise when that angel called him a "mighty warrior" and said, "God has chosen you to save Israel!"

BE A HERO!

Have you ever thought you weren't good enough to serve God—to lead that prayer or talk to your friend about Jesus? Don't believe it! God's heroes don't have superpowers. They're simply willing to let the One who does have superpowers work through them.

Gideon didn't believe he was the right man for the job. You see, Israel was being oppressed yet again, this time by the Midianites. The Midianites were mean, and there were a lot of them! So Gideon asked God for a sign—just to be sure. Actually, he asked for two signs—just to be extra sure. God gave him those signs. First, God made a piece of wool wet when it should have been dry. Then He made the wool dry when it should have been wet. At last, Gideon believed. And God gave him victory over the Midianites, just as He said He would.

It's easy to think the people of the Bible were superheroes. But, really, they were ordinary people who had doubts and fears. The heroes of the Bible were simply willing to follow God. God will do great things through people who let Him use them—including you. ▶JUDGES 6–7

HERO TRAINING Read 2 Timothy 1:7. Did God create you to be afraid? No! But that doesn't mean you'll never be afraid. It does mean you don't have to let fear stop you from serving God. Remember that He'll always be there to help you be strong and brave (Isaiah 41:10).

GIDEON STRUGGLED TO BELIEVE HE WAS THE RIGHT MAN FOR THE JOB. HE ASKED GOD FOR A SIGN.

IF TOMORROW THIS FLEECE IS WET WITH DEW, THEN I KNOW GOD WILL SAVE ISRAEL.

THE NEXT MORNING, THE FLEECE WAS WET, BUT THE GROUND WAS DRY.

STILL, GIDEON ASKED FOR ONE MORE SIGN.

Never Too Late

Samson—God's Strong Man

JOB: 12TH JUDGE OF ISRAEL

NOTABLE WOMEN IN SAMSON'S LIFE: HIS WIFE, WHO WAS A PHILISTINE WOMAN FROM TIMNAH (A CITY IN CANAAN), AND DELILAH, WHO WAS A BEAUTIFUL WOMAN FROM THE VALLEY OF SOREK

KEY TERM: NAZIRITE: A PERSON WHO MADE A SPECIAL PROMISE TO SERVE GOD BY FOLLOWING CERTAIN RULES, INCLUDING NOT CUTTING ONE'S HAIR

"The Lord is a God who shows mercy and is kind. The Lord doesn't become angry quickly. The Lord has great love and faithfulness."

—EXODUS 34:6 ICB

Imagine you were given an amazing gift, and you only had to follow one rule to keep it. But you broke that one rule. How badly would you want a second chance to make things right?

God gave Samson, a Nazirite, a gift of unbelievable strength. Samson was so strong that he once killed a lion with his bare hands. To keep his strength, Samson only had to honor God by never cutting his hair. For years, Samson kept that rule (though he didn't always honor God in other ways). As Israel's judge, he used his great strength to defend God's people against their enemies, the Philistines.

Then Samson fell in love with a Philistine woman named Delilah. She didn't care about honoring God like Samson did. So the Philistine leaders bribed Delilah—they would give

her money if she could discover the secret of Samson's strength. Delilah agreed, and she begged and pestered Samson for the answer.

Finally, Samson couldn't stand it anymore. "If you cut my hair," he said, "I'll lose my strength." The next thing Samson knew, he was both bald and blind in a Philistine prison.

Then one day Samson was brought to the Philistine temple. There, he begged God for a second chance to obey Him and defend the Israelites against God's enemies. God heard him and gave Samson the strength to bring the temple down on the Philistines.

No matter how many mistakes you make or how many rules you break, it's never too late to call out to God. When you do, He'll give you a second chance too. ▶JUDGES 16

☥ HERO TRAINING God knows you will make mistakes. That's why He sent Jesus, the only perfect person. Check out Romans 5:8 and Luke 19:10. It's never too late to ask God for a second chance.

Wherever You Go

Ruth—The Loyal

MEANING OF NAME:
"COMPANION" OR
"FRIEND"

MOTHER-IN-LAW:
NAOMI

FIRST HUSBAND:
MAHLON

Ruth said, "Don't ask me to leave you! Don't beg me not to follow you! Every place you go, I will go. Every place you live, I will live. Your people will be my people. Your God will be my God."

—RUTH 1:16 ICB

*L*oyal is a word you probably don't hear often. But when you think about what loyal means—to be faithful, to stick with someone no matter what—it's easy to see why being loyal is so important. After all, how great is it to know that you have someone you can always count on?

Ruth was loyal to Naomi, especially when times got tough. Years earlier, Naomi, her husband, and their two sons had moved from Israel to Moab to escape a terrible famine. But things were not easy for the family in Moab either. First, Naomi's husband died. Then her sons died. Naomi was alone in a foreign country with only her sons' Moabite wives, Ruth and Orpah, to help her.

Naomi decided to return home to Israel. She urged her daughters-in-law to return to their own families. Orpah did, but Ruth refused. Naomi was Ruth's family now. Ruth knew life in Israel would be hard. (Israelites and Moabites were enemies.) But her loyalty to Naomi was greater than her fears. She would not leave Naomi alone.

A loyal person is one of this world's greatest treasures. And loyalty is a treasure that grows even richer when you give it away. Seek loyal friends, and be a loyal friend in return.
▶*RUTH 1*

🏃 **HERO TRAINING** God rewarded Ruth's love and loyalty by making her part of Jesus' family tree. Read Matthew 1 and find the women who were ancestors of Jesus. What made each of them so special that they were listed in Jesus' family tree?

🦸 BE A HERO!

Heroes don't leave friends to face hard times alone. Sometimes you can help fix a problem; sometimes you can't. But you can be there. Share hugs, listen, visit. Just *be there*. It's more important than you might think.

A New Beginning

Ruth—The Redeemed

Everyone goes through hard times. Sometimes you make a mistake and have to deal with the consequences. Sometimes bad things just happen. Hard times will come and go. When you're in the middle of one, it can feel as if you'll never be happy again, that life will never be good again. But that's simply not true.

RUTH AND NAOMI WERE POOR. ONE DAY RUTH WENT OUT INTO THE FIELD TO COLLECT SOME LEFTOVER GRAIN. THE FIELD BELONGED TO BOAZ, WHO SAW RUTH GLEANING THE SEEDS.

BOAZ APPROACHED RUTH AND TOLD HER SHE WAS WELCOME ON HIS LAND.

I WOULD LIKE TO GATHER THE SHEAVES AFTER THE HARVESTERS.

YOU ARE VERY WELCOME TO COLLECT WHATEVER YOU WANT.

AND HELP YOURSELF TO SOME WATER IF YOU ARE THIRSTY.

SECOND HUSBAND: BOAZ

SON: OBED

DESCENDANTS: KING DAVID AND JESUS; RUTH IS ONE OF ONLY FIVE WOMEN LISTED IN THE FAMILY HISTORY OF JESUS (MATTHEW 1)

He has given me a new song to sing, a hymn of praise to our God. Many will see what he has done and be amazed. They will put their trust in the LORD.
—PSALM 40:3 NLT

BOAZ AND RUTH GOT MARRIED AND HAD A CHILD NAMED OBED.

Ruth had been through a terrible time. Her husband had died. Then she had followed her mother-in-law, Naomi, to a new country filled with strange people and strange ways. In addition, Naomi and Ruth were very poor. To get food, Ruth went into the fields to search for bits of grain dropped by farm workers. Yet Ruth never gave up. And God never forgot her.

As it turned out, the fields Ruth gathered grain in belonged to Boaz, a relative of Naomi. He noticed Ruth and asked others about her. When Boaz discovered who Ruth was and all she had done for Naomi, he wanted to marry her. But first, Boaz bought back the land that had once belonged to Naomi's family. He redeemed both Ruth and Naomi by paying the debt they couldn't pay and setting them free from poverty.

God will redeem you too. When you love and follow Him. He will pay for your sin and give you a place with Him—not just in heaven but also here on earth. ▶ *RUTH 2–4*

🕴 BE A HERO!

When Boaz first noticed Ruth, he helped her by giving her food. Ask your parents to help you prepare a meal for someone who is struggling through a difficult time. Then deliver it with a smile and a prayer!

🕴 HERO TRAINING Because we all sin, we all owe a debt to God. It's a debt so huge that we can never pay it on our own. That's why God sent Jesus—to pay that debt for us. Read Colossians 1:14 and 1 Peter 1:18–19. How did Jesus redeem us?

The Power of Prayer

Hannah—A Praying Woman

MEANING OF NAME: "FAVOR" OR "GRACE"

HUSBAND: ELKANAH

CHILDREN: SAMUEL, PLUS THREE OTHER SONS AND TWO DAUGHTERS (1 SAMUEL 2:21)

I took my troubles to the LORD; I cried out to him, and he answered my prayer.

—PSALM 120:1 NLT

Look outside. What do you see—sky, birds, or trees? From the hugeness of space to the tiniest ant, God made everything. And just think, that's the same powerful God who listens when you pray. When you're hurting or sad, do you remember to turn to God—the most powerful One?

Hannah remembered. Hannah was heartbroken because she had no children. One day she slipped away to pray at the Lord's house. Tears falling down her face, she poured out her heart to God: "Dear Lord, if You give me a son, I'll make sure he serves You all his life."

Eli, the priest, watched Hannah. Though her lips moved, no sound came out. Eli went over to Hannah, and she explained that she was praying for God's help. Eli said, "May God give you what you asked for." Hannah returned home, no longer sad.

The Lord heard Hannah's prayer, and He gave her just what she wanted. God blessed her with a son, Samuel. When Samuel was old enough, Hannah kept her promise. She returned to the Lord's house and left Samuel with Eli to serve the Lord.

When you're sad or hurting or unsure of what to do, remember to turn to God. He doesn't always give us what we want, but He always listens and always helps. ▶ *1 Samuel 1–2*

🏃 HERO TRAINING When Jesus died on the cross, He opened the throne room of heaven to us. That means you can step right into the presence of God—anytime, anywhere. And you can talk to Him about anything. Just take a look at Hebrews 4:16. God wants to hear from you!

🦸 BE A HERO!

The prayers of a believing person are powerful. So just imagine how powerful the prayers of a whole group of believing people are! Start a prayer group with your friends. Meet on the playground at school or on the weekends in your neighborhood.

AFTER THE BOY IS WEANED, I WILL TAKE HIM AND PRESENT HIM BEFORE THE LORD, AND HE WILL LIVE THERE.

I PRAYED FOR THIS CHILD, AND THE LORD HAS GIVEN ME WHAT I ASKED FOR. SO NOW I AM GIVING HIM TO THE LORD.

A Voice in the Night

Samuel—Who Listened to God

Have you ever been talking to someone and then realized he or she wasn't listening to anything you said? How did that make you feel? Okay, now be honest. Have you ever been that person who didn't really listen? To listen is to give someone your time, attention, and interest. And it's so important—especially when God is the One doing the talking.

Samuel discovered that truth when he was a young boy. He grew up in the Lord's house with Eli, the priest. One night Samuel awoke when he heard his name called: "Samuel!" He

MEANING OF NAME:
"NAME OF GOD"

MOTHER: HANNAH

FATHER: ELKANAH

Samuel said, "Speak, for your servant
is listening."

—1 SAMUEL 3:10 NIV

thought it was Eli and ran to him. "Here I am," Samuel said. "You called me." But Eli hadn't called, and he sent the boy back to bed. Twice more Samuel heard his name called in the night, and twice more he ran to Eli.

At last Eli realized what was happening—the Lord was calling Samuel! So Eli told the boy what to do. The next time the Lord called, Samuel answered as Eli had told him: "Speak, for your servant is listening." Samuel kept on listening to the Lord all the days of his life.

BE A HERO!

Listening is a skill that takes practice. The first step is to stop whatever else you're doing (including figuring out what you want to say next) and just *listen*. Look the person in the eye. Ask questions to make sure you understand. Real heroes really listen.

God still speaks to us today, though you probably won't hear a voice calling your name in the night. He now speaks mostly through His Word. So when you open your Bible or sit down to hear a Bible lesson, make sure you're really listening. Let Samuel's words be your prayer: "Speak, Lord, for Your servant is listening." ▶ *1 SAMUEL 3*

HERO TRAINING You can listen to God's voice in the pages of His Word anytime you want. The more you read His Word, the more easily you'll recognize His voice. Read John 10:27–28. What promise does God give to people who listen to His voice?

THE LORD CALLED SAMUEL TWO MORE TIMES, AND AGAIN SAMUEL THOUGHT IT WAS ELI WHO WAS CALLING.

MY BOY, IT MUST BE THE LORD CALLING YOU! IF HE CALLS AGAIN, ANSWER AND SAY YOU ARE HIS SERVANT.

THE LORD CAME AND CALLED THE BOY AGAIN.

SAMUEL! SAMUEL!

YOUR SERVANT IS LISTENING, LORD!

GOD GAVE SAMUEL AN IMPORTANT MESSAGE THAT NIGHT, AND SOON ALL OF ISRAEL RECOGNIZED SAMUEL AS A PROPHET OF THE LORD. GOD CONTINUED TO SPEAK TO SAMUEL THROUGHOUT HIS LIFE.

A King for Israel

Samuel—The King Maker

Have you ever wanted something just because everyone else had it? Maybe it was a special kind of bike or a game or a cool jacket. You begged and pleaded for it until, at last, it was yours! But once you had it, you realized it wasn't so great after all.

That's exactly what happened to the people of Israel. You see, they had been ruled by judges for years. Samuel was the latest judge, but he was growing old. The Israelite leaders told Samuel they wanted a king to rule them, just like all the other nations had.

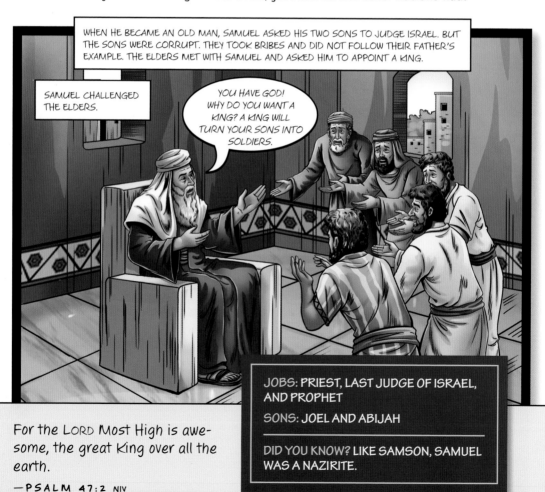

WHEN HE BECAME AN OLD MAN, SAMUEL ASKED HIS TWO SONS TO JUDGE ISRAEL. BUT THE SONS WERE CORRUPT. THEY TOOK BRIBES AND DID NOT FOLLOW THEIR FATHER'S EXAMPLE. THE ELDERS MET WITH SAMUEL AND ASKED HIM TO APPOINT A KING.

SAMUEL CHALLENGED THE ELDERS.

YOU HAVE GOD! WHY DO YOU WANT A KING? A KING WILL TURN YOUR SONS INTO SOLDIERS.

JOBS: PRIEST, LAST JUDGE OF ISRAEL, AND PROPHET

SONS: JOEL AND ABIJAH

DID YOU KNOW? LIKE SAMSON, SAMUEL WAS A NAZIRITE.

For the LORD Most High is awesome, the great King over all the earth.

—PSALM 47:2 NIV

"But you have God!" Samuel exclaimed. "Why do you want a king? He'll take your sons for soldiers and your daughters for servants. He'll take your best fields and make you his slaves!"

The Israelites wouldn't listen. So God told Samuel to anoint Saul, a young warrior, as Israel's first king. And just like Samuel warned, King Saul took advantage of the people. And that was just the beginning of Israel's troubles with kings.

BE A HERO!

Wanting to be like everyone else is dangerous. God's heroes know they were created to be different. Stand up for what's right, help the weak, and—most important of all—make God the ruler of your life.

The Israelites wanted a king so badly that they didn't care whether a king would be good or bad. It's easy to get caught up in wishing for something you don't have. But don't let that thing become "king" of your life. God is the only true King! ▶1 SAMUEL 8–10

HERO TRAINING Idols are things people worship instead of God. It's easy to look at a statue and think it's silly to worship such things. But look at Matthew 4:8–10. Satan tempted Jesus with riches and power. Those are still pretty tempting idols today. What was Jesus' answer in verse 10? That's exactly what your answer should be too!

GOD TOLD SAMUEL HE WOULD GUIDE HIM IN SELECTING A MAN TO BE THE HEBREWS' FIRST KING.

SAMUEL SOON MET A YOUNG WARRIOR NAMED SAUL, WHO WAS LOOKING FOR THE DONKEYS HIS FATHER HAD LOST. GOD TOLD SAMUEL THAT THIS WAS THE MAN WHO SHOULD BE KING.

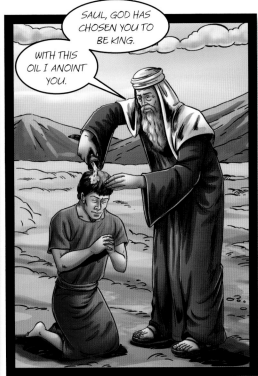

SAUL, GOD HAS CHOSEN YOU TO BE KING.

WITH THIS OIL I ANOINT YOU.

Big Trouble!

David—The Giant Slayer

FIRST JOB: SHEPHERD

FATHER: JESSE

SIBLINGS: SEVEN BROTHERS AND TWO SISTERS

GREAT-GRANDMOTHER: RUTH, THE MOABITE

The LORD is for me; I will not fear; what can man do to me?

—PSALM 118:6 NASB

GOLIATH CHARGED AT DAVID...

...BUT DAVID NEVER WAVERED. HE PLACED A SMOOTH STONE IN HIS SLINGSHOT AND LET IT FLY.

Just because you are young doesn't mean you don't have troubles. Some will be big and some not so big. But when you follow God, you don't have to be afraid of those troubles. God is on your side, and He can knock even the biggest troubles down to size.

David was just a young shepherd when he went to visit his brothers in the Israelite army. The Israelites were gathered on one side of a great valley, while their enemies, the Philistines, were gathered on the other side. The Philistines had a champion named Goliath. At nine feet, nine inches tall, he was enormous! Morning and evening, he dared the Israelites to send one man to fight him. But no one would go.

When David arrived, he heard Goliath's challenge. "I will fight him!" David declared. God had already helped David defend his sheep against lions and bears. David knew God would help him against this fierce enemy as well. Armed with only his staff, his sling, and some stones, David ran out to meet Goliath. With a few swings of his sling, he let the first stone fly. *BAM!* Goliath was dead.

David wasn't afraid to face Goliath because he knew he didn't go into battle alone. God was on his side. Whether you're facing a giant bully, an enormous test, or a Goliath of a problem, God will be with you too! ▶*1 Samuel 17*

🐾 BE A HERO!

Heroes face troubles together with God. They help others face troubles with God too. Think of someone who's dealing with some sort of trouble. Pray for that person each day until the troubles are past. Give him or her a card that says you're praying.

🏃 **HERO TRAINING** God is always with His people. Look up Zephaniah 3:17 and think about the answers to these questions: Where is God? Is He strong or weak? Will He save you? And because He loves you so much, what will He do?

Friends Forever

Jonathan—A True Friend

THE KING HELD A FEAST FOR THE NEW MOON CELEBRATION.

WHERE IS DAVID? WHY IS HE NOT HERE?

DAVID BEGGED ME TO LET HIM GO TO BETHLEHEM FOR A FAMILY GATHERING.

REBELLIOUS SON! YOU ARE MORE LOYAL TO DAVID THAN TO ME! AS LONG AS HE IS ALIVE, YOU WILL NEVER BE KING!

FATHER: KING SAUL
SON: MEPHIBOSHETH
BEST FRIEND: DAVID

A friend loves you all the time, and a brother helps in time of trouble.

—PROVERBS 17:17 NCV

There are all kinds of friends. There are friends you hang out with at lunch or who are good for a pickup game of basketball. There are fair-weather friends who stick around as long as things are fun and easy. And then there are true friends—the ones who are there for you, no matter what.

Jonathan was a true friend to David, even though they were an unlikely pair. Jonathan was King Saul's son, and he should have been king after his father. But God had chosen David to be Israel's next king. Jonathan and David should have been enemies. Instead, they were best friends.

When King Saul became jealous of David and tried to kill him, Jonathan warned David to run. "Go in peace," Jonathan said. "We have promised in the Lord's name that we will be friends. We will keep this promise between us and our descendants forever." Years later, after Jonathan was killed and David was crowned king, David kept that promise. He brought Jonathan's son to the palace to live with him.

True friends are a rare treasure and a blessing from God. The best way to find that kind of friendship is to be a true friend yourself—through thick and thin, just like David and Jonathan. ▶1 SAMUEL 18–20

🐟 BE A HERO!

What is your definition of a true friend? How would that person act in good times and in tough times? What would he or she do when you're happy or when you're sad? Write out what you think a true friend should be like. Now go and be that friend.

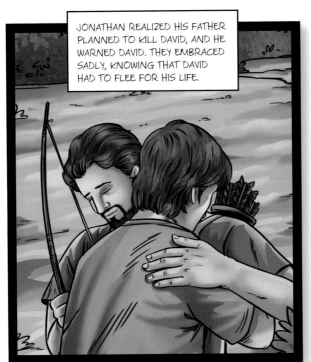

JONATHAN REALIZED HIS FATHER PLANNED TO KILL DAVID, AND HE WARNED DAVID. THEY EMBRACED SADLY, KNOWING THAT DAVID HAD TO FLEE FOR HIS LIFE.

🏃 **HERO TRAINING** You may have some really good friends, but there is only one perfect friend—God! He's always with you, even in the tough times (Psalm 23:4). He's always ready to listen (Psalm 145:18). And He's always willing to help (Psalm 46:1). And the best part is that anyone can be close to Him. James 4:8 says, "Come near to God, and God will come near to you" (ICB). So take a moment to talk with God, your perfect friend, today!

A Welcome Gift

Abigail—The Hospitable

Chances are, someone has been hospitable to you. Hospitality means making someone feel welcome—in your home, at your lunch table, or in your circle of friends. And doesn't it feel wonderful to be welcome?

There was a time when David was not feeling welcome. David and his men were camping in the wilderness, near the flocks of a man named Nabal. While they were there, they protected Nabal's sheep from bandits. So when David heard Nabal was having a feast, he thought he would be welcome.

But the ungrateful Nabal said, "Who is David? Why should I give him any food?" David was furious. He gathered his men to attack.

FIRST HUSBAND: NABAL, WHOSE NAME MEANS "FOOL"

SECOND HUSBAND: DAVID

Do not forget to do good and to share with others.
—HEBREWS 13:16 NIV

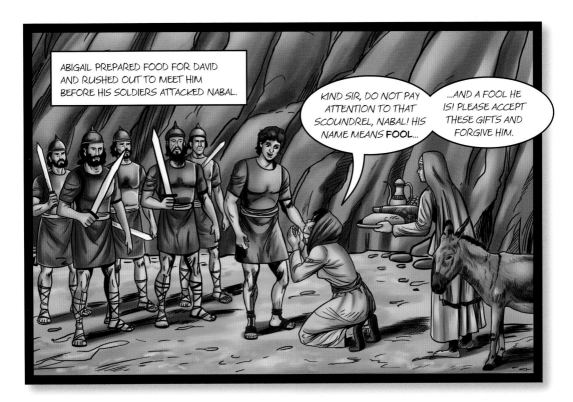

Fortunately, Nabal was married to a wise woman named Abigail. Abigail rode out to meet David. And she brought heaps of food with her. Abigail begged David to accept her gift and spare her family. David was touched by her kindness. And he was glad she had stopped him from killing in anger.

With Abigail's gifts, David and his men returned to camp peacefully. Nabal, on the other hand, heard what happened and dropped like a stone from fear. He died ten days later. Afterward, Abigail became David's wife.

Abigail saved the day with hospitality. Your own welcoming gift of friendship just might save someone's day. Open your heart to those around you today! ▶1 Samuel 25

♟ BE A HERO!

Hospitality has the power to break down walls, soften hearts, and turn strangers into friends. Look for opportunities to make people feel welcome. Take dinner to a new neighbor. Ask someone to sit with you at lunch. Or invite someone who lives alone to be a part of your next family dinner.

🏃 HERO TRAINING Read Revelation 3:20. Is Jesus welcome in your life? Are you glad to meet Him in His Word, to talk to Him every day in prayer, to introduce your friends to Him? How can you make Jesus welcome in every moment of your life?

The One True King

David—A Man After God's Own Heart

Have you ever been honored for something you did? Perhaps you won an art competition and your talents were honored with a blue ribbon. Or maybe you hit the winning home run and were honored with the game ball. To honor someone is to treat him or her with great respect.

David honored God throughout his life. After King Saul died, there was a terrible war for the throne. David was thirty years old when, at last, he became king of Israel. But there were still more battles, and David honored God by following His instructions on who and when to fight.

AFTER SAUL'S DEATH, TWO PEOPLE CLAIMED THE THRONE OF ISRAEL. THERE WAS DAVID AND ISHBOSHETH, ANOTHER OF SAUL'S SONS. NOT LONG AFTER SAUL DIED, THE TWO MEN AND THEIR ARMIES BATTLED EACH OTHER. THE WAR OVER WHO WOULD RULE ISRAEL LASTED A LONG TIME. MANY WERE KILLED.

HOMETOWN: BETHLEHEM

WIVES: MICHAL, ABIGAIL, BATHSHEBA, AND MANY OTHERS

WHERE: JERUSALEM, WHERE HE BUILT A GREAT PALACE

Honor the LORD for his glory and strength. Honor the LORD for the glory of his name. Worship the LORD in the splendor of his holiness.

—PSALM 29:1-2 NLT

In addition to fighting the nation's battles, David also warred with his own selfishness and sin. He made lots of mistakes. He did lots of things God told him not to do. But through it all, David loved God. David always came back to Him. David knew that the Lord was the true King of Israel and of his life. That's why God Himself called David "a man after my own heart" (Acts 13:22 NIV).

Will you try to honor God with every word, every thought, and every action? Yes, you'll make mistakes. Sometimes you'll choose to do what you want even though you know God's ways are best. But if you come back to God and let Him rule over your life, then you, too, will be a person after God's own heart.

▶ *2 SAMUEL 2–6*

🏃 BE A HERO!

One way to honor God is to honor those who serve Him. Bake brownies for your minister. Deliver goodie bags to the church secretary and cleaning crew. Write a card thanking your Bible teacher for helping you learn to honor and obey God.

🏃 HERO TRAINING How can you honor God in your life? It's no secret—God's Word tells you how! You can honor God by telling others about Him (Psalm 75:1), singing praises to Him (Psalm 95:1–2), and obeying Him (2 John 1:6).

DAVID WAS GOD'S WARRIOR. HE BATTLED THE PHILISTINES AND DEFEATED THEM SEVERAL TIMES. HE DEFEATED THE ARAMEANS, THE EDOMITES, AND OTHER ENEMIES. DAVID FOUGHT BACK HADADEZER, KING OF ZOBAH.

GOD'S LIGHT AND FAVOR TRULY SHINED ON DAVID.

A Terrible Sin

David—The Repentant

Y ou messed up—big-time. You did what you knew you weren't supposed to do. Then, instead of admitting your mistake, you tried to cover it up. Of course, you got caught. Then you were in even bigger trouble than before! Has that ever happened to you?

It happened to David. Yes, King David, that man after God's own heart, messed up—big-time. It all started when he spotted a beautiful woman and invited her to his palace. Her name was Bathsheba. The problem was that she was married to one of David's warriors. When Bathsheba became pregnant, David tried to cover up his sin by ordering her husband to the front of

AGE: 30
YEARS OLD
WHEN HE
BECAME KING
OF ISRAEL

REIGN: 40
YEARS

God, be merciful to me because you are loving. Because
you are always ready to be merciful, wipe out all my wrongs.
Wash away all my guilt and make me clean again.
—PSALM 51:1-2 ICB

the battle lines, where he was killed. David then married Bathsheba himself and thought everything was all right.

But God knew what David had done. He sent the prophet Nathan to tell David a story about two men: a rich man, who had many animals, killed a poor man's only lamb for a feast. David was outraged—until he realized he was like the rich man in the story. As king, David had wealth and power. He had stolen from someone with much less. David begged God to forgive Him, and God did.

The fact is, everyone sins. Sometimes it's by accident, and other times it's on purpose. Don't try to cover up your sin. That only makes it worse. Talk to God. Tell Him you're sorry, and ask Him to forgive you. He always will.
▶ *2 SAMUEL 11–12*

🏃 HERO TRAINING

Confession is telling God that you know what you did was wrong. It's agreeing with God that it was a sin. Repentance is being sad about that sin and doing your best not to sin again. Read 1 John 1:9 and Acts 3:19 to find out what wonderful thing happens when you confess and repent.

❦ BE A HERO!

Everyone messes up sometimes. But heroes aren't too proud to admit when they are wrong. Whether you've wronged God, your parents, a friend, or someone else, go and tell them you're sorry. And then do your best to make it right.

YES, YES, I *UNDERSTAND!* **I HAVE SINNED! FORGIVE ME, LORD! PLEASE FORGIVE ME!**

THE LORD FORGAVE DAVID.

Sing to the Lord!

David—Singer and Songwriter

DESCENDANT: JESUS

KNOWN FOR: BEING A MAN AFTER *GOD'S OWN HEART* (ACTS 13:22)

DID YOU KNOW? DAVID PLAYED THE LYRE (A KIND OF HARP) AND WROTE ABOUT HALF OF THE 150 PSALMS.

Let all that I am praise the LORD; with my whole heart, I will praise his holy name.

—PSALM 103:1 NLT

Are there days that make you want to sing with joy? King David often expressed his feelings with songs. But he didn't just sing when he was joyful.

David loved to make music. When he was a young man, he sang and played the harp for King Saul. David's songs often soothed Saul's troubled soul.

David wrote many songs, or psalms. At least seventy-three songs in the book of Psalms are his. He wrote some of them when he was still a shepherd. He wrote others when he was running for his life from Saul and still others when he was finally king. He wrote when he was happy, sad, thankful, and angry. No matter what was happening, David's songs always praised and worshipped the Lord.

Worship isn't just singing, though. Worship is declaring that the Lord is worthy of being praised. It's making God the greatest treasure of your heart and life. Jesus gave one of the best definitions for worship: "Love the Lord your God with all your heart and with all your soul and with all your mind" (Matthew 22:37 NIV).

Whether you sing it, say it, or write it, worship the Lord! There is no other God. Only He is worthy of worship and praise.

▶ THE BOOK OF PSALMS

🏃 HERO TRAINING David praised and sang to the Lord no matter what he was feeling. Read Psalm 22, Psalm 57, and Psalm 95. What was David feeling in each psalm? How can David's words teach you to always sing praises to the Lord?

🦸 BE A HERO!

Heroes worship God, and they help others worship Him too. Gather a group of friends together and sing praises, help set up for worship time at your church, or offer to clean up after. Or write praises on colored squares of paper and then string them together to make a banner that you hang up.

Asking for Wisdom

Solomon—The Wise King

FATHER: KING DAVID

MOTHER: BATHSHEBA

WRITER: SOLOMON WROTE SONG OF SOLOMON, PROVERBS, AND ECCLESIASTES

If any of you needs wisdom, you should ask God for it. God is generous. He enjoys giving to all people, so God will give you wisdom.

—JAMES 1:5 ICB

What if you could ask for anything and you knew you would get it. What would you ask for? Money? Friends? Fame? Power? Solomon was given a chance to do just that. He was promised anything he wanted. And not from someone here on earth but from God. What he asked for just might surprise you.

After King David died, Solomon became king of Israel. God came to Solomon in a dream and said, "Ask for whatever you want Me to give to you." Solomon could have asked for great wealth or power or for a long life. But he didn't ask for any of those things. Instead, Solomon asked for the wisdom to lead God's people. Wisdom is knowing the right thing to do or say at the right time. The Lord was so pleased with Solomon's request that He not only gave him wisdom but also health and wealth and power.

In those days, there was no one equal to Solomon. And there has never been a person since as wise as he was. But don't think the gift of wisdom was just for Solomon. In James 1:5, God promises that if you ask Him for wisdom, He will give it to you too. He might not send it all at once, but He will give exactly what you need when you need it. ▶ *1 KINGS 2–3*

🕴 BE A HERO!

Being wise isn't about being a know-it-all. In fact, it's just the opposite. An important part of wisdom is knowing when you *don't* have the answer. Heroes aren't afraid to ask for help, to listen to what others have to say, and—most importantly—to talk to God about it.

🏃 **HERO TRAINING** Solomon filled the book of Proverbs with his godly wisdom. Start each morning by reading a proverb. Keep a list of your favorite ones or underline them in your Bible.

ALL I ASK FROM YOU IS WISDOM SO I MIGHT RULE WELL.

I WILL GIVE YOU WHAT YOU ASKED FOR, AND I WILL GIVE YOU WHAT YOU DID NOT ASK FOR! THERE WILL BE NO KING IN THE WORLD AS GREAT AS YOU!

GOD WAS PLEASED WITH SOLOMON'S ANSWER...

...AND ALONG WITH WISDOM GAVE HIM RICHES, HONOR, GREATNESS, AND LONG LIFE.

All for God

Solomon—The Builder

BUILDING A GREAT TEMPLE IN JERUSALEM TO HOUSE THE ARK OF THE COVENANT WAS ONE OF DAVID'S DREAMS. BUT GOD HAD DELAYED THE CONSTRUCTION UNTIL ALL THE WARS WERE OVER AND SOLOMON TOOK POWER.

Imagine you're cleaning your room, but no one is coming to see it. How hard do you work? Do you dust every corner? Or do you stuff a few things under your bed? Now imagine your grandparents are coming to visit, and they're going to stay in your room. Do you work a little harder?

The more special someone is to you, the harder you'll work to please him or her. That probably explains why King Solomon worked so hard, and spared no expense, when it came to building a temple for God.

Solomon wanted only the best for God. He hired stonecutters to chisel blocks for the temple walls. He bought expensive wood to line the walls and

WHEN: SOLOMON DEDICATED THE TEMPLE AFTER SEVEN YEARS OF CONSTRUCTION

KEY TERM: ARK OF THE COVENANT: A BOX THAT HELD HOLY OBJECTS, SUCH AS THE TEN COMMANDMENTS AND A JAR OF MANNA. THE BOX WAS COVERED IN GOLD AND HAD TWO SCULPTURES OF CHERUBIM, OR ANGELS, ON THE TOP.

Whatever you do, work at it with all your heart, as working for the Lord, not for human masters.

—COLOSSIANS 3:23 NIV

WHEN THE TEMPLE WAS FINISHED, BOTH THE INSIDE AND OUTSIDE WERE MAGNIFICENT.

form the roof. He had artists carve trees and gourds, cherubim and flowers. And he had the inside of the temple coated in pure gold. It was magnificent!

When the temple was finished, the priests placed the ark of the covenant inside, in the Holy of Holies. Then the glory of the Lord filled the temple in a cloud. Solomon finished his great task by praying and making sacrifices to dedicate the temple to the Lord. It had taken seven years and a fortune in gold and silver to build. Only the best was good enough for God.

That's what God wants from you too. Not a temple, but the best of your life. God wants the best of your time, your talents, and your love. Because He gave Jesus—His best—to you. ▶ *1 Kings 6–8*

🏃 **HERO TRAINING** So often we waste our time worrying. We worry about what to eat, what to wear, and how to get what we want. But look at what Jesus says in Matthew 6:33. If we'll give the best of our time and energy to God, He'll take care of everything else.

🦸 BE A HERO!

Colossians 3:23 tells us to do everything as if we're doing it for God. So whatever heroic things you tackle today—whether it's cleaning your room, helping a younger child with homework, or visiting a sick friend—do it as if you were doing it for God. Because you are.

A Widow's Faith

The Widow of Zarephath—The Baker

Imagine you woke up late and skipped breakfast so you wouldn't miss the bus. Lunch is hours away, and your stomach is rumbling like an earthquake. Finally, it's time to eat. But your best friend forgot his lunch. How hard would it be to share? What if it wasn't your best friend but a total stranger?

In the city of Zarephath, there lived a widow and her son. There was a terrible drought, and food was hard to get. When Elijah came to the city, the widow was gathering sticks for

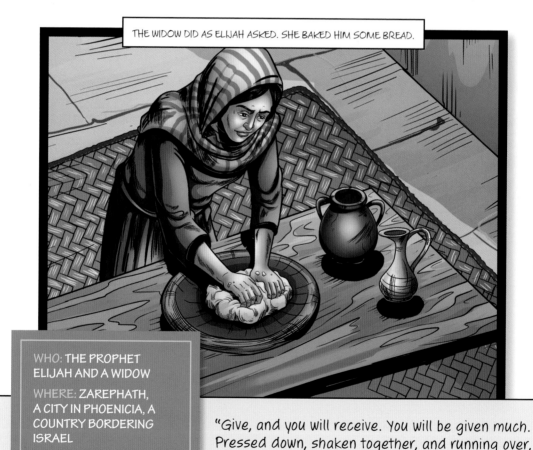

THE WIDOW DID AS ELIJAH ASKED. SHE BAKED HIM SOME BREAD.

WHO: THE PROPHET
ELIJAH AND A WIDOW

WHERE: ZAREPHATH,
A CITY IN PHOENICIA, A
COUNTRY BORDERING
ISRAEL

WHEN: DURING THE REIGN
OF KING AHAB OF ISRAEL

"Give, and you will receive. You will be given much. Pressed down, shaken together, and running over, it will spill into your lap. The way you give to others is the way God will give to you."

—LUKE 6:38 NCV

a fire. She planned to use her last bit of oil and flour to bake some bread. Then she and her son would have no more food to live on.

So when Elijah asked the widow for bread, it was no small request. But his request came with a promise from God: if the widow gave Elijah the bread, her oil and flour would not run out until the rain came again. The widow did as Elijah asked. She baked the bread and gave it to him. And God kept His word—just as He always does. There was food every day for Elijah, the woman, and her son.

BE A HERO!

Being a hero isn't about getting attention. It's about giving, especially to those who can't give back. When your next birthday rolls around, throw a party for local foster kids or those in a homeless shelter.

Through Elijah, God asked the widow to give all that she had. It wasn't much, but God made it enough. There will come a time when God will ask you to give all you have—your money, time, or even your food. Remember the widow and know that God will make what you give enough.

▶ *1 Kings 17*

🏃 **HERO TRAINING** Think about the words of Luke 6:38. No matter how much you give, you can't out give God. His gifts might not be money or things, but you can be sure that they'll be amazing! The next time you give, pay attention to all the ways God gives back to you.

ELIJAH ATE THE BREAD, AND AS HE HAD PROMISED...

...THERE WAS STILL FLOUR IN THE JAR AND OIL IN THE JUG! AND AS LONG AS THE DROUGHT CONTINUED, THERE WAS ALWAYS FLOUR IN THE JAR AND OIL IN THE JUG.

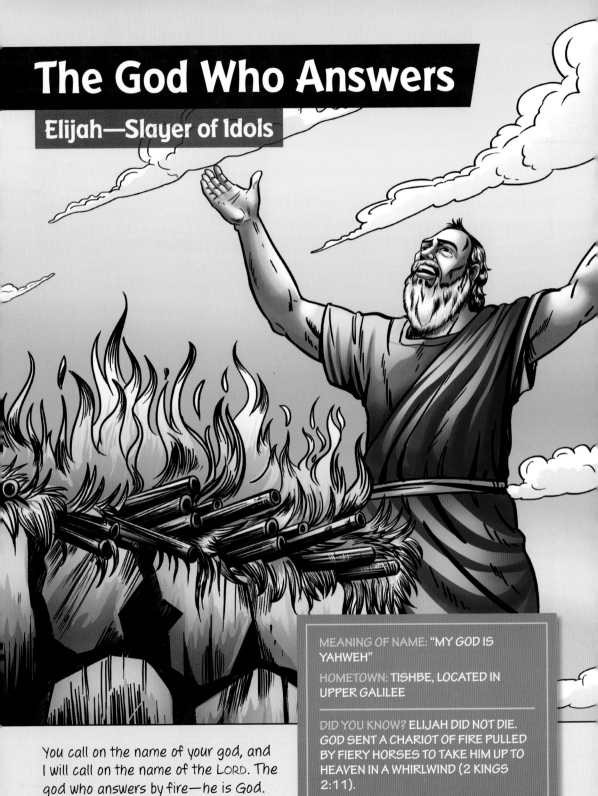

The God Who Answers

Elijah—Slayer of Idols

MEANING OF NAME: "MY GOD IS YAHWEH"

HOMETOWN: TISHBE, LOCATED IN UPPER GALILEE

DID YOU KNOW? ELIJAH DID NOT DIE. GOD SENT A CHARIOT OF FIRE PULLED BY FIERY HORSES TO TAKE HIM UP TO HEAVEN IN A WHIRLWIND (2 KINGS 2:11).

You call on the name of your god, and I will call on the name of the LORD. The god who answers by fire—he is God.

—1 KINGS 18:24 NIV

Do you really know who God is? Do you know how amazing and powerful He is? It's easy to let God become just another Bible story character. But He's so much more than that. He is Lord of all!

The people of Israel had forgotten who God really is. You see, Ahab was the new king of Israel, and he was as wicked as they come. He led the people in worshipping the false god Baal.

So one day the prophet Elijah challenged Ahab: "Bring all the prophets of Baal, and meet me on Mount Carmel." The people gathered to see the showdown. Elijah asked for two bulls and wood to burn the sacrifices on. "You call on your god, and I will call on the Lord," Elijah said. "The god who answers by fire is the one true God."

Baal's 450 prophets went first. From morning to evening, they shouted, danced, and prayed to Baal. But not a spark flashed on the woodpile.

Then it was Elijah's turn. First, he dug a trench around the stone altar and laid the wood and bull on top. Next, he had water poured over everything until it ran off the altar and filled the trench. "Answer me, Lord!" Elijah called. Instantly, fire shot from heaven and burned up the bull and wood and even the stones and water. "The Lord is God!" the people said.

And He still is! Lots of idols and false gods try to steal your time and attention, but remember: there is only one God who answers the prayers of His people—the Lord God!

▶ *1 Kings 18*

🏃 HERO TRAINING In today's world, a lot of people say it's okay to worship whatever god you want—or no god at all. But there is one true God. Read about the power and might of God in Job 38–39. There is no other "god" who can do all that the Lord can do!

BE A HERO!

Even good things can become idols. Don't let anything—sports or friends or video games—steal your time and attention from God. Make sure your day includes time to talk to God, read His Word, and praise Him. Real heroes put God first.

"Send Me!"

Isaiah—The Willing

MEANING OF NAME: "THE LORD HAS SAVED"

BIRTHPLACE: JUDAH

FATHER: AMOZ

WHEN: ABOUT 700 YEARS BEFORE JESUS WAS BORN

Then I heard the Lord's voice. He said, "Whom can I send? Who will go for us?" So I said, "Here I am. Send me!"

—ISAIAH 6:8 ICB

Your mom asks you to unload the dishwasher. Your dad needs help in the yard. Your teacher asks you to help another student with a tricky problem. Chances are, you'd say yes to all these requests—because you don't really have a choice, right? But what about your attitude? Do you want to help? Or does your attitude show you'd rather be doing something else?

God wants His people to help. But even more than that, He wants His people to want to help. Like Isaiah did.

One day Isaiah was in the temple when suddenly he saw the Lord seated on His throne. Angels hovered above Him, singing His praises. Isaiah was terrified! He knew he was a sinner. There was no way he could be in the presence of such a holy God and still live. An angel flew down to him and touched his lips with a burning coal. "Your sins are taken away," the angel said.

Then the Lord Himself called out, "Who is willing to be My messenger?"

"Here I am," Isaiah answered. "Send me!"

God used Isaiah to send a message to His people. Isaiah went on to become one of God's greatest prophets—all because He was willing to help. When you are willing to let God use you, He'll do great things with your life too! ▶ISAIAH 6

🏃 **HERO TRAINING** When God called Samuel, Samuel said, "Speak, Lord. I am your servant, and I am listening" (1 Samuel 3:10 ICB). When God called Isaiah, Isaiah said, "Here I am. Send me!" Though you may not hear a voice the way Samuel and Isaiah did, God is calling you to do His work too. Write out your answer to God.

🏃 BE A HERO!

Your willingness to help can make all the difference in your life and in the lives of others. Practice your volunteer spirit today. When someone asks for help, say, "Here I am. Send me!"

81

Shaped by God

Jeremiah—The Reluctant Prophet

MEANING OF NAME: "THE LORD LIFTS UP"

JOB: PROPHET, FOR OVER 40 YEARS

FATHER: HILKIAH, A HIGH PRIEST

PLACE OF DEATH: EGYPT

"You are like the clay in the potter's hands."
—JEREMIAH 18:6 ICB

Have you ever made a mistake—a really big one? Then afterward, you felt as if there was no hope of ever making things right again? Perhaps you said something mean to a friend and thought, *I bet they'll never forgive me for that.*

The people of Israel made a really big mistake—the worst kind, actually. They turned away from God. But God didn't give up on them. He called Jeremiah to speak to the people for Him.

But Jeremiah was a little reluctant. That means he was not sure he was willing to do it. After all, he was young, and he didn't know what to say.

But God promised to tell Jeremiah exactly what to say. Then He sent him to the potter's house. There Jeremiah saw the potter making a pot from clay. Something went wrong with the pot, but the potter didn't toss out the clay. Instead, he used that same clay to make a better pot. The potter reshaped the clay until it was just the way he wanted it.

The Lord said to Jeremiah, "Tell the people I am like the potter and they are the clay. I can shape them into a strong nation. Or, if they don't stop their evil ways, I can reshape them and start again."

When we make mistakes, God doesn't give up on us and toss us away. He reshapes us with His own hands to be just the way He wants us to be. ▶*JEREMIAH 18*

☠ **HERO TRAINING** Shape a piece of Play-Doh into a little pot, just as Jeremiah watched the potter do. Now take a closer look at it. Do you see your fingerprints all over it? In the same way, when you let God reshape your heart by following His Word, He leaves His fingerprints all over you (2 Corinthians 3:18)!

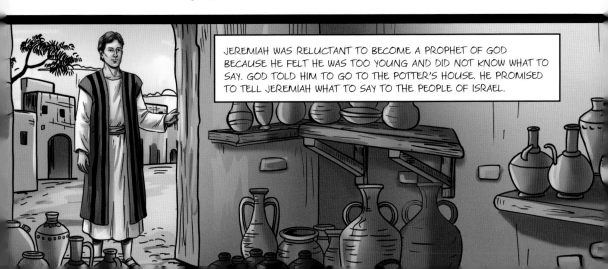

JEREMIAH WAS RELUCTANT TO BECOME A PROPHET OF GOD BECAUSE HE FELT HE WAS TOO YOUNG AND DID NOT KNOW WHAT TO SAY. GOD TOLD HIM TO GO TO THE POTTER'S HOUSE. HE PROMISED TO TELL JEREMIAH WHAT TO SAY TO THE PEOPLE OF ISRAEL.

Praise and Problems
Job—The Sufferer

MEANING OF NAME: "THE PERSECUTED ONE" (IN HEBREW); "REPENTANT ONE" (IN ARABIC)

HOMETOWN: THE LAND OF UZ

FRIENDS: ELIPHAZ, BILDAD, AND ZOPHAR

The Lord gave these things to me. And he has taken them away. Praise the name of the Lord.

—JOB 1:21 ICB

Have you ever had a day that you thought would never end? Not only did you wake up late; you missed the bus. You lost your homework, and just when things couldn't possibly get worse, you got grounded for something you didn't even do!

Multiply that by about a zillion, and you'll begin to understand how Job felt. You see, Job was a good man who followed God in everything he did—and God blessed him for it. Job had seven sons and three daughters. He owned great herds of sheep and cattle, thousands of camels, hundreds of oxen, and much more.

WHEN HE HEARD HOW MUCH HE HAD LOST, JOB RIPPED OFF HIS COAT...

...CUT OFF HIS HAIR, AND FELL TO HIS KNEES.

BUT HE STILL TRUSTED GOD.

But Satan told God that Job loved Him only because of the blessings. "Take everything away and see if he still worships You," Satan challenged.

"Very well," God said. So Satan went to work.

Raiders ran off with Job's oxen and donkeys. They killed his servants and stole his camels. A terrible storm killed all his children. Painful sores covered Job from head to toe. Even his wife said, "You should curse God and die!"

But Job trusted God: "We take the good things from God. Should we not take the bad things too?" he asked.

The fact is, the Devil is still at work in this world, stirring up all kinds of suffering. And our own sins only make things worse. But no matter how hard the bad times get, God will always see us through—as Job was about to find out.
▶ *Job 1–2*

🗡 HERO TRAINING Read Matthew 7:24–27 about the wise man and the foolish man. Notice that the storm came into both men's lives. There will always be troubles (2 Timothy 3:12). How will building your life on God help you stand strong when storms of trouble come?

🕴 BE A HERO!

Bad days happen to everyone. If you keep reading about Job, you'll see that his friends only made things worse. They said that he deserved all those terrible things! When a friend is having a rotten day, don't blame her. Encourage and pray with her.

A Great Reward

Job—The Restored

BECAUSE JOB WAS A GOOD AND FAITHFUL MAN, GOD RESTORED HIS RICHES.

HIS FRIENDS DINED WITH HIM AND CONSOLED HIM FOR ALL THE TRIALS HE HAD ENDURED.

LIFESPAN: ABOUT 200 YEARS

DID YOU KNOW? WHEN JOB'S FRIENDS FIRST SAW JOB AND HIS SUFFERING, THEY DIDN'T SPEAK FOR SEVEN DAYS AND NIGHTS (JOB 2:13).

Anyone who wants to come to him must believe that God exists and that he rewards those who sincerely seek him.

—HEBREWS 11:6 NLT

magine: you wake up one morning, and nothing is the same. Your home and family car have been taken away. Your parents lost their jobs. To make things worse, your whole body is covered with itchy, burning bumps. Sounds like a nightmare, doesn't it? For Job, it was a nightmare come true.

Job had lost everything: his children, his riches, his health. And he didn't understand why. While Job asked God why all this was happening to him, he still trusted God to see him through. "I know You can do all things," he said to the Lord.

At last, God rewarded Job's faith. God healed the sores on his face and body and took away all the pain. God restored Job's riches. Family and friends visited and comforted Job. God blessed him with fourteen thousand sheep, six thousand camels, a thousand yoke of oxen, and a thousand donkeys—twice as much wealth as Job had before. God also gave Job ten more children. Job lived to see his many grandchildren and great-grandchildren. He died old, content, and still trusting and loving the Lord.

Tough times come to everyone, even to people who love and trust God. We may not understand why bad things happen or how it will all work out. But we can know that the Lord will bless those who love Him.
▶ JOB 42

🕴 BE A HERO!

Most likely, there are people in your community who feel a lot like Job. They have lost everything. We often call them *homeless*. Put together simple care packages with a bottle of water, a snack, and a pair of socks or gloves, along with an encouraging Bible verse. Keep them in your family's car to give to those in need.

🏃 **HERO TRAINING** Read Isaiah 55:8–9. Is it possible to understand God's ways? Now, read Jeremiah 29:11. Even though we may not understand God's plans for us, what does He promise about them?

GOD BLESSED JOB WITH MORE ANIMALS AND CHILDREN.

HE ALSO BLESSED JOB WITH MANY GRANDCHILDREN AND GREAT-GRANDCHILDREN. JOB DIED OLD, CONTENT, AND TRUSTING AND LOVING THE LORD.

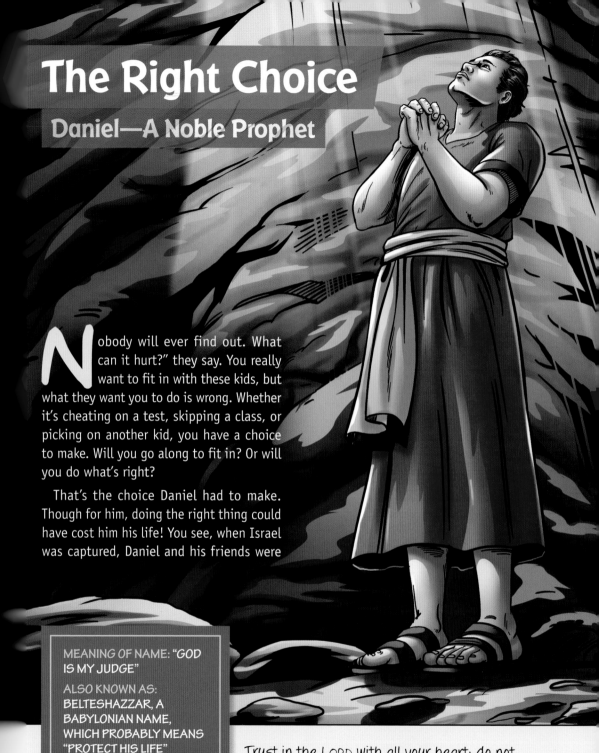

The Right Choice

Daniel—A Noble Prophet

"Nobody will ever find out. What can it hurt?" they say. You really want to fit in with these kids, but what they want you to do is wrong. Whether it's cheating on a test, skipping a class, or picking on another kid, you have a choice to make. Will you go along to fit in? Or will you do what's right?

That's the choice Daniel had to make. Though for him, doing the right thing could have cost him his life! You see, when Israel was captured, Daniel and his friends were

MEANING OF NAME: "GOD IS MY JUDGE"

ALSO KNOWN AS: BELTESHAZZAR, A BABYLONIAN NAME, WHICH PROBABLY MEANS "PROTECT HIS LIFE"

WHEN: DANIEL WAS TAKEN CAPTIVE AROUND 605 BC

Trust in the LORD with all your heart; do not depend on your own understanding. Seek his will in all you do, and he will show you which path to take.
—PROVERBS 3:5–6 NLT

carried away to Babylon. The young men like Daniel were brought to the palace and trained to help the Babylonian king, Nebuchadnezzar. They were treated well and were even given the same food as the king. But that was the problem. God's laws said they couldn't eat that kind of food.

Daniel and his friends had a choice to make: disobey God or risk the king's anger by refusing his food. Daniel's guard didn't want to change anything. He'd be in trouble if they got sick. But Daniel convinced him to try serving them only vegetables and water for ten days. After those ten days, Daniel and his friends were healthier than all those who had eaten the king's food.

It would've been easy for Daniel to simply eat the king's food. It was only food, right? Wrong! It was disobeying God. Always choose to do right, even in the small things and even when no one else will know. ▶ DANIEL 1

🏃 **HERO TRAINING** Take a closer look at today's verse. When you're faced with a choice, what should you seek? What does God promise when you do?

DANIEL AND HIS FRIENDS WERE WELL-EDUCATED AND CAME FROM NOBLE FAMILIES IN JERUSALEM. THE KING LOOKED AFTER THEM WELL. HE BROUGHT THEM TO THE PALACE TO LIVE AND LEARN ABOUT BABYLON. THEY WERE ALSO GIVEN THE SAME FOOD AS THE KING, AND THIS CAUSED A PROBLEM.

WE CANNOT EAT THIS RICH FOOD OR DRINK THIS WINE.

BUT IF YOU DON'T EAT PROPERLY, YOU WON'T BE FIT AND STRONG, AND THE KING WILL PUNISH ME!

DANIEL PERSUADED THE STEWARD TO LET THEM EAT VEGETABLES AND WATER FOR 10 DAYS. AT THE END OF THAT TIME, THE STEWARD WAS AMAZED TO FIND THE YOUNG MEN HEALTHIER THAN THOSE WHO ATE THE KING'S FOOD.

Facing the Lions

Daniel—The True

What are you known for? Maybe it's your sense of humor, your kindness, or your bright red hair. What about your faith? Are you known for your faith in God?

Daniel was. After King Nebuchadnezzar's rule ended, Daniel went on to serve the new king, Darius. He was so pleased with Daniel's work that he planned to put him in charge of all the other officials. Those other officials didn't like that one bit, though, and they set out to trap Daniel.

EVEN WHEN IT WAS AGAINST THE LAW, DANIEL PRAYED TO GOD THREE TIMES A DAY.

WHO: DANIEL, KING DARIUS, LIONS, AND AN ANGEL

WHEN: AROUND 539 BC

DID YOU KNOW? A LIONS' DEN WAS A PIT WITH A SMALL OPENING AT THE TOP, MAKING IT IMPOSSIBLE FOR A PRISONER TO ESCAPE.

"You should be a light for other people. Live so that they will see the good things you do and will praise your Father in heaven."

—MATTHEW 5:16 NCV

THE MORNING AFTER DANIEL WAS THROWN IN THE LIONS' DEN, DARIUS RAN TO THE DEN. HE WAS OVERJOYED TO FIND DANIEL ALIVE.

The officials tricked Darius into making a new law: for thirty days people could only pray to the king. Anyone caught breaking the law would be thrown into a lions' den!

Daniel knew about the law. But he still went to his room and knelt to pray, just as he had always done. The officials, of course, hurried to tell the king.

King Darius was heartbroken, but even he couldn't change a law once it was written. As Daniel was thrown into the lions' den, Darius called out, "May your God rescue you!" And He did! God sent an angel to close the lions' mouths. And Darius wrote a new law that said everyone must respect the God of Daniel.

Daniel didn't charge into battle or knock down a giant. He simply knelt to pray, just as he'd always done. But his faithful action gave God an opportunity to show His power. Your faithful actions can do the same. Show God to the world by showing how much you love Him.

▶DANIEL 6

🏋 BE A HERO!

When you tell the world you follow Jesus, be ready for the world to start watching you. When your team loses, when you flunk the test, or when a friend gossips about you, be sure your words and actions show the world who your Lord is!

🏃 **HERO TRAINING** Read Darius's new law in Daniel 6:25–27. Daniel's faith and God's miracle helped the king realize who the true God is. How powerful is your faith to those around you?

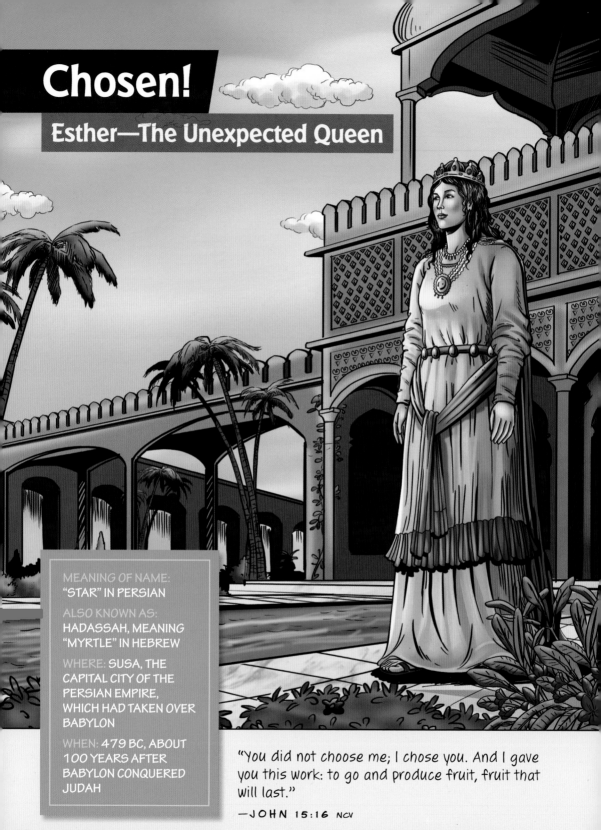

Chosen!

Esther—The Unexpected Queen

MEANING OF NAME:
"STAR" IN PERSIAN

ALSO KNOWN AS:
HADASSAH, MEANING
"MYRTLE" IN HEBREW

WHERE: SUSA, THE
CAPITAL CITY OF THE
PERSIAN EMPIRE,
WHICH HAD TAKEN OVER
BABYLON

WHEN: 479 BC, ABOUT
100 YEARS AFTER
BABYLON CONQUERED
JUDAH

"You did not choose me; I chose you. And I gave
you this work: to go and produce fruit, fruit that
will last."

—JOHN 15:16 NCV

WHEN AHASUERUS SAW ESTHER, HE FELL IN LOVE. HE MARRIED HER AND MADE HER QUEEN.

magine trying out for a part in a play. You expect to be a tree, only required to stand on the side and wave your arms. Instead, you find yourself in the starring role!

It's probably safe to say that Esther never expected to be starring in the role of queen of Persia. She was a Jewish orphan living with her uncle when King Ahasuerus decided to find a new queen. All the beautiful young women in the land were brought to the king's palace, including Esther. As she left for the palace, Uncle Mordecai gave Esther a warning. She was to tell no one she was a Jew, because some people did not like the Jews.

After a year of beauty treatments, Esther finally met the king. Ahasuerus fell in love and married her. Esther was now the queen.

If this were a fairy tale, the story would end right there, with a happily ever after. But it isn't a fairy tale. It's the true story of what happened to Esther and to God's people. That story—and Esther's part in it—was just beginning.

Esther was chosen by God to play a starring role in the story of her people. And guess what! God has chosen you for a starring role too—in the story of His kingdom. Follow Him and find out what your part will be!
▶ ESTHER 1–2

🔱 BE A HERO!

Whatever role God chooses for you, do it with all your might. Today it could be babysitting, so be the best babysitter ever. Tomorrow it could be serving the homeless, leading a prayer, or being a missionary across the world. Whatever your role, be a star for God!

🔥 HERO TRAINING Esther's plans for her life probably didn't include being queen of Persia, but God had other plans. You probably have some plans for your day, your week, and your life. Check out Proverbs 16:9. Are you ready to follow God's plans for you?

Saving the Day!

Esther—The Brave

Have you ever come face-to-face with a monster-size problem? Maybe you thought, *I can't do anything about that. It's just too big!* Maybe it was a problem with a bully, a parent's job, or a friend's sickness. Whatever it was, you felt as if you couldn't help at all.

That's probably how Esther felt when she found out about Haman's evil plan. Haman, one of King Ahasuerus's most powerful officials, hated the Jewish people. He convinced the king to order that all the Jews be killed. (Remember, Esther hadn't told anyone she was Jewish!)

WHATEVER YOU ASK OF ME SHALL BE GRANTED.

I WOULD LIKE YOU TO COME WITH HAMAN TO A BANQUET I WILL PREPARE.

HUSBAND: KING AHASUERUS

UNCLE: MORDECAI

DID YOU KNOW? THE JEWISH FEAST OF PURIM CELEBRATES ESTHER AND GOD'S DELIVERANCE OF THE JEWISH PEOPLE FROM HAMAN.

Who knows, you may have been chosen queen for just such a time as this.
—ESTHER 4:14 NCV

Esther's uncle, Mordecai, asked Esther to go to the king and save her people. But Esther was afraid. If she went to the king without being called for, she could be killed. And the king hadn't called for Esther in a long time! But Mordecai told her, "Who knows, you may have been chosen queen for just such a time as this."

Esther prayed and fasted. Then she went to the king. Her prayers were answered! Haman's evil plan was stopped, and the Jewish people were saved. All because Esther was brave enough to play the part God had given her.

BE A HERO!

When you find yourself thinking, Somebody should help, be that somebody. When you say, "Somebody should do something," do something yourself. Sometimes you'll fix the whole problem; other times you'll fix only a part. And sometimes you might not seem to help at all. But God sees His heroes in action, and He smiles.

There will be times when you think you can't make a difference. That's the time to reach out and pray to the One who's big enough to tackle any trouble. Then play the part God gives you.

▶ *ESTHER 3–9*

HERO TRAINING You were created to make a difference—just check out Ephesians 2:10. Now, you might find yourself thinking, I'm too young to make a difference for God. Don't believe it! Just look at 1 Timothy 4:12.

HAMAN AND THE KING ATTENDED QUEEN ESTHER'S BANQUET.

WHATEVER YOU ASK, QUEEN ESTHER, I SHALL GRANT YOU.

I BEG YOU TO SPARE THE LIVES OF MY PEOPLE, FOR SOMEONE HAS PLOTTED TO WIPE US OUT.

WHO WOULD DO SUCH A THING?

IT IS *HAMAN!*

Nowhere to Hide

Jonah—The Runaway Prophet

Have you ever gotten so sick of chores, homework, and all the other no-fun stuff that you thought it might be nice to run away from it all?

That's what Jonah thought. You see, God had a job for Jonah. "Go to Nineveh," God said. "Tell the people to repent."

But Jonah didn't want to go. He didn't think the people of Nineveh deserved a second chance. So he ran away. God said

HOMETOWN: GATH HEPHER, JUST NORTH OF NAZARETH AND WEST OF THE SEA OF GALILEE

WHERE: GOD TOLD JONAH TO GO TO NINEVEH, AN ASSYRIAN CITY, BUT JONAH BEGAN TRAVELING IN THE OPPOSITE DIRECTION, TO TARSHISH

"I am a God who is near," says the Lord. "I am also a God who is far away. No one can hide where I cannot see him. . . . I fill all of heaven and earth."

—JEREMIAH 23:23-24 ICB

to go east, but Jonah got on a boat headed west. He soon found out, however, that running away from God wasn't so easy.

When the boat set sail, God sent a terrible storm. The sailors tried everything to save themselves. At last, Jonah told the sailors the storm was his fault for disobeying God. "Throw me into the sea," he said, "and save yourselves." The sailors didn't want to do that! But when the storm got worse, they tossed Jonah into the sea.

BE A HERO!

You can't run from God, but you can run for Him. Run (or walk) a 5K race to support a cause that helps people. Because heroes don't run away. They run to help.

The storm stopped, and an enormous fish popped up and swallowed Jonah in a single gulp! For three days, Jonah sat in that fish's belly. Then Jonah prayed. God heard, and the fish spat him out. This time, when God told Jonah to go to Nineveh, Jonah went.

It took three days inside a stinky fish for Jonah to learn he couldn't run away from God. And neither can you. That's a good thing, though! It means wherever you go, God is right there with you. ▶*Jonah 1–4*

HERO TRAINING Read Psalm 139:7–12. Is there anywhere you can hide from God? Is there anywhere you can go that God is not already there? Now read Deuteronomy 31:8 to discover why this is such a wonderful thing!

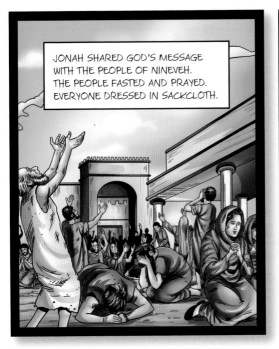

JONAH SHARED GOD'S MESSAGE WITH THE PEOPLE OF NINEVEH. THE PEOPLE FASTED AND PRAYED. EVERYONE DRESSED IN SACKCLOTH.

EVEN THE KING WORE RAGS AND REPENTED. GOD SAW HOW THE CITY HAD TURNED AWAY FROM EVIL. GOD SAID HE WOULD SPARE THE CITY.

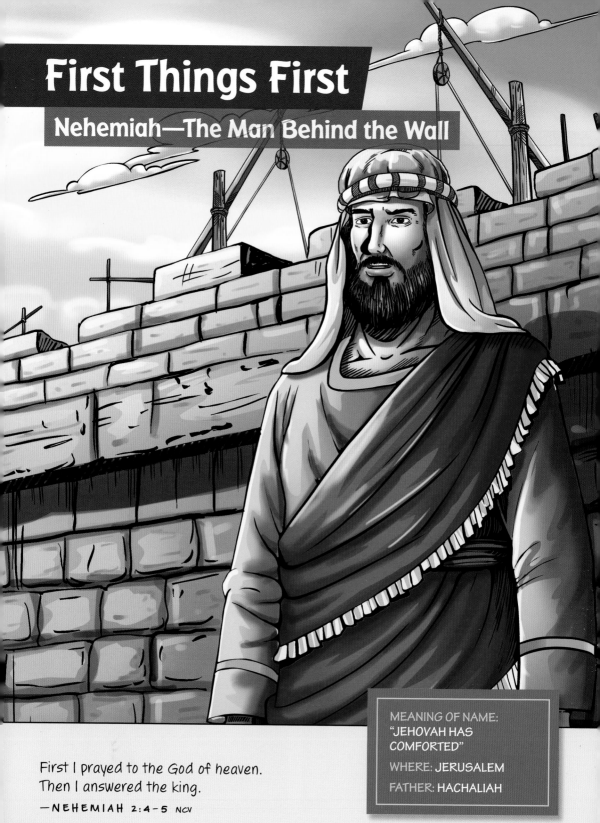

First Things First

Nehemiah—The Man Behind the Wall

First I prayed to the God of heaven.
Then I answered the king.

—NEHEMIAH 2:4–5 NCV

MEANING OF NAME:
"JEHOVAH HAS
COMFORTED"

WHERE: JERUSALEM

FATHER: HACHALIAH

WHEN THE WORK BEGAN, WORKERS FIRST CLEARED THE FALLEN STONES AWAY...

...AND REPLACED THEM WITH NEW STONES.

Let's say that you have a huge project to do. Perhaps it's a big report for school or a puppet show for church. What's the first thing you do? Do you make a list of supplies or round up people to help?

Nehemiah had a huge project ahead of him: rebuilding the walls around Jerusalem to keep the people safe from attacks. He didn't start with a list of supplies, though. He didn't ask for workers. The first thing he did was pray. With God leading the way, amazing things began to happen.

First, the king of Persia gave Nehemiah permission to return to Jerusalem, and the king helped Nehemiah get the supplies. Once Nehemiah reached Jerusalem, all the people got to work. They cleared the fallen stones away and replaced them with new stones. When their enemies planned to attack and stop the rebuilding, Nehemiah divided the people into two groups. Half worked on the wall while the other half stood guard. With God's help, the entire wall was rebuilt in just fifty-two days! God's people were safe.

Notice what Nehemiah did first: he prayed. When you're facing something big, it's tempting to start with what you can do yourself. Instead, remember Nehemiah and start with God. With God leading the way, amazing things will happen! ▶*NEHEMIAH 1–7*

🏃 HERO TRAINING Build a wall of prayer around your day. Before your feet hit the floor, ask God to guide your steps. As you wash your hands, ask God to wash your sins away. When you eat, ask God to make you strong. And as you close your eyes, ask God to guard your sleep. How many other "stones" can you add to your wall of prayer?

🦸 BE A HERO!

Heroes are often busy. It can be tough to find time to stop and pray every time you need to. Try "rocket" prayers. These quick, short prayers "blast" straight from your heart to God's ear. They can be as quick and simple as, "Help me, Lord!" or "Show me what to do!" or "Be with me."

Powerful Words

Ezra—The Priest

MEANING OF NAME: "HELPER"

JOBS: PRIEST AND SCRIBE (SOMEONE WHO WROTE AND ORGANIZED BIBLICAL TEXTS)

FATHER: SERAIAH (A DESCENDANT OF AARON, MOSES' BROTHER)

Your word is a lamp to guide my feet and a light for my path.

—PSALM 119:105 NLT

Have you ever read a book that made you laugh out loud? Or cry? Words are powerful things. And no words are more powerful than those of the Bible. They're the words of God!

Ezra knew the power of God's words. But in his time, the people of Jerusalem were not following God's laws. They even worshipped false gods! Ezra was so heartbroken by this that he prayed, "Lord, I am sorry! I apologize for the people of Jerusalem. They have sinned against you!"

One day, after Nehemiah had helped rebuild Jerusalem's walls, all the people gathered to celebrate a holy festival. There, Ezra read from the Book of the Law. Many people were upset as they realized how much they had sinned. But Nehemiah said, "Friends, do not be sad! This is a holy day—a day to rejoice! We must have a feast and make sure the poor have plenty to eat." So the people celebrated. And for seven days Ezra read from the Book of the Law. God's words were so powerful that, by the end of the feast, everyone promised to love and obey God.

Ezra knew that if the people would truly listen to God's Word, it would change their lives. God's Word is still powerful today. And when you truly listen, it will change your life too.

▶ *Ezra 9–10; Nehemiah 8*

🏃 HERO TRAINING

Reading God's Word is a powerful thing, and reading it out loud can make it really come to life. Pick your favorite passage and read it out loud to your parents, to your friends, or simply to yourself. If you can't think of a favorite passage, start with Psalm 23.

🏃 BE A HERO!

God's Word is like a seed. You plant it, and God makes it grow. Plant seeds of His Word by hiding verses for others to find. Write your favorite verses on cards. Then tuck them into library books, leave them on friends' desks, or hide them around the house for your family.

EVERYONE CAME TOGETHER IN ONE OF THE CITY SQUARES. THERE, EZRA READ FROM THE BOOK OF LAW OF MOSES. MANY WERE UPSET BY THEIR SINS.

FRIENDS, DO NOT BE SAD! THIS IS A HOLY DAY—A DAY TO REJOICE!

WE MUST HAVE A FEAST AND MAKE SURE THE POOR HAVE PLENTY TO EAT.

SO THE PEOPLE CELEBRATED.

A Willing Heart

Mary—Blessed by God

Have you ever been startled by an opportunity to serve God or help His people? Perhaps your parents asked you to teach a Bible lesson all on your own. Maybe your pastor asked you to lead a prayer for the whole church, or your friends asked you to explain a Bible story to them. It was the last thing you were expecting, and it was a little bit scary!

Mary would understand. A visit from the angel Gabriel was almost certainly the last

WHERE: **THE SMALL TOWN OF NAZARETH, LOCATED IN MODERN-DAY ISRAEL**

FIANCÉ: **JOSEPH**

ANCESTOR: **KING DAVID**

DID YOU KNOW? **THE ANGEL GABRIEL ALSO VISITED DANIEL (DANIEL 9).**

Mary responded, "I am the Lord's servant. May everything you have said about me come true."

—LUKE 1:38 NLT

thing she was expecting that day. And learning that she would be the mother to God's own Son was shocking news! Mary was surprised and confused and afraid. But her answer shows why God chose her for such an important role.

Mary didn't make excuses for why she couldn't do as God asked. She didn't try to figure out an easier way. Yes, she asked questions. But they weren't the doubting or get-somebody-else kind. Mary simply answered, "I am the Lord's servant. May everything you have said about me come true." Then she praised God with a song.

Whenever you're asked to do something for God or His people, remember Mary. Let her answer be yours too: "I am the Lord's servant!" God will help you do whatever He asks of you.

▶ LUKE 1

🏃 HERO TRAINING Mary was chosen by God because she loved Him and her heart was willing to serve Him in whatever way she could. You have also been chosen by God to serve Him, and that service begins in your heart. Read Colossians 3:12–13. What kind of heart does God want you to have? Spend some time memorizing these Bible verses so you'll always remember what a serving heart looks like.

🕯 BE A HERO!

What God asked Mary to do was way outside her comfort zone. Why not step out of your comfort zone too? If you've never taught a Bible lesson, ask someone to help you learn. If you've never shared your faith with your friends, give it a try. Heroes are brave enough to try something new!

An Unlikely King

Jesus—The Savior

MARY AND JOSEPH TRAVELED TO BETHLEHEM, THE CITY OF JOSEPH'S ANCESTOR DAVID.

THEY STOPPED AT AN INN TO REST.

MY WIFE IS ABOUT TO GIVE BIRTH! ARE YOU SURE THERE ARE NO ROOMS?

I AM SORRY, FRIEND. BUT THERE IS A STABLE IN THE BACK.

YOU CAN STAY THERE.

The angel said to them, "Do not be afraid. I am bringing you good news that will be a great joy to all the people. Today your Savior was born in the town of David. He is Christ, the Lord."

—LUKE 2:10–11 NCV

MEANING OF NAME: "GOD SAVES"

BIRTHPLACE: BETHLEHEM

MOTHER: MARY

EARTHLY FATHER: JOSEPH

f you were king of the world, where would you live? Would you build a palace dripping with gold or a massive mansion with a sparkling pool? Would there be servants, fancy clothes, and the best of everything? That's what the world would expect. But Jesus—the King of all creation—wasn't a rich ruler. He was different, right from the start.

God had long promised His people a Savior, and the Jews expected that God would send a mighty king who would overthrow their Roman rulers. They did not expect someone like Jesus.

⚡ BE A HERO!

Angels brought the good news of Jesus' birth to the shepherds (Luke 2:8–14). How can you announce the good news of Jesus? Write it on a card. Write a simple poem. Make up a song. Heroes let the world know that Jesus is born!

Jesus didn't come with political power, great riches, or a vast army. He came as a helpless baby. He was born to a humble young woman who married a carpenter from the lowly village of Nazareth.

Jesus wasn't even born in a house. A census forced Mary and Joseph to travel to Bethlehem, and a too-crowded inn meant that our Savior was born in a stable. There was no cradle of gold, only a feeding trough. There was no palace filled with servants, only an audience of shepherds and

a band of angels singing in the night. This tiny baby wasn't at all what the people expected. But He was going to change everything!

Jesus doesn't care about riches or power. He cares about serving His Father and saving His people. Let those two things guide your life, and live like Jesus!

▶ MATTHEW 1; LUKE 2

WHILE MARY WAS IN THE STABLE, SHE GAVE BIRTH TO A SON. SHE WRAPPED HIM IN SWADDLING CLOTHS AND LAID HIM IN A MANGER.

🏃 HERO TRAINING It's easy to get caught up in wanting the latest and greatest that everyone else seems to have. But God says those things aren't important—not for His Son and not for you. Take a look at Deuteronomy 6:5 to see what God says is most important of all.

Celebrate!

The Wise Men—Worshippers of the King

THE THREE WISE MEN LEFT HEROD AND TRAVELED TO BETHLEHEM, GUIDED BY THE STAR.

How does your family celebrate birthdays? Perhaps you have your favorite meal and a cake. Maybe friends and family join in. And, of course, there are probably presents! While there are big parties and small parties, there has never been a celebration quite like the one for Jesus the King.

WE HAVE TRAVELED GREAT DISTANCES TO SEE THIS CHILD.

ALSO KNOWN AS: MAGI, WHICH MEANS "WISE MEN"

WHERE: A HOUSE IN BETHLEHEM

WHEN: AFTER THE BIRTH OF JESUS

KEY TERM: FRANKINCENSE AND MYRRH: EXPENSIVE SPICES WORTHY OF A KING

Come, let us bow down in worship, let us kneel before the LORD.
—PSALM 95:6 NIV

When Jesus was born in Bethlehem, a bright star appeared in the sky. In an eastern country, some wise men saw the star. They knew it was a sign that the King of the Jews—the Savior—had been born. They wanted to celebrate His birth, so they traveled toward the star for many, many miles.

In Jerusalem, they met with the evil King Herod. He pointed the wise men toward Bethlehem, hoping they would lead him to the new king. But Herod didn't want to worship Jesus. He wanted to kill Him!

When the wise men found Jesus, He was no longer a baby. He was a young boy, living in a house with Mary and Joseph. Seeing Jesus, the wise men bowed down and worshipped. They gave Him valuable gifts of gold, frankincense, and myrrh. Then, having been warned in a dream not to go back to Herod, they returned to their country by a different way.

The wise men traveled from far away to celebrate Jesus, but you don't have to travel at all! You can celebrate His birth and His promises anytime and anywhere. ▶ MATTHEW 2

🏃 **HERO TRAINING** Celebrating, or worshipping, Jesus is about more than singing songs and praises (though that's important too). It's living a life that honors Him in everything you do. Check out Colossians 3:14–17 for ways to worship Jesus your whole life through.

109

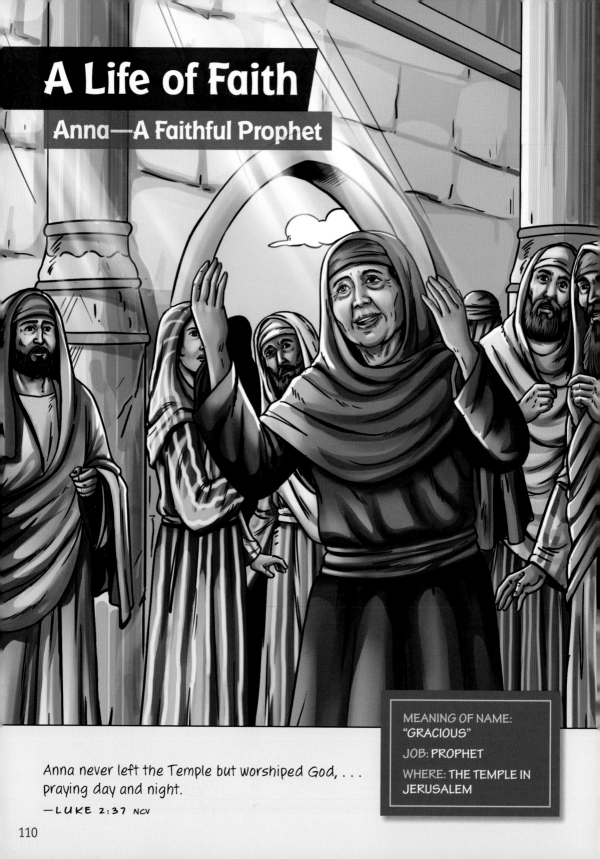

A Life of Faith

Anna—A Faithful Prophet

Anna never left the Temple but worshiped God, . . . praying day and night.

—LUKE 2:37 NCV

MEANING OF NAME: "GRACIOUS"

JOB: PROPHET

WHERE: THE TEMPLE IN JERUSALEM

Have you ever met an older person—perhaps a grandparent, neighbor, or someone from your church—who just shines with the love of Jesus? That person tries to follow Jesus in everything. And just to be around him or her makes you feel wonderful. That's the kind of love and faith that comes from a life spent following Jesus.

Anna had that kind of love and faith. After her husband died when she was still a young woman, she lived the rest of her life at the temple. As a prophet of God, she spent her days praying and fasting and worshipping.

🦸 BE A HERO!

Some followers of God are not able to go to church. Why not take church to them? Gather your family, your friends, or your Sunday school class. Go and visit those who are unable to leave their houses or those staying in a nursing home. Sing, read the Bible, and worship God with them.

When Joseph and Mary brought baby Jesus to the temple to dedicate Him to God, Anna, of course, was there. She was now an old woman, and God rewarded her lifetime of faith. Anna saw the Savior with her own eyes. As she peeked at the baby, Anna gave thanks to God. Then she told everyone there about Jesus, that He was the One who would rescue Jerusalem.

Anna spent her whole life loving and worshipping God, and it showed. When you spend your life loving and worshipping God, the light of the Lord's love will shine through you too!
▶ LUKE 2

___

🦸 HERO TRAINING It's easy to say, "Be a faithful follower of Jesus." But what does that really mean? What does that look like on a Tuesday morning in class or a Friday night on the basketball court? Read Romans 12:9–21 to see what faithfully following God should look like in your life.

In His Father's House

Jesus—The Student

Have you ever gotten separated from your parents? Perhaps your family was at the park and you ran to the swings while they unpacked the car. Or maybe you were at the beach and you left your parents' side to check out a cool seashell. You weren't really worried because you knew exactly where you were and what you were doing. But your parents didn't know those things, and they were worried sick!

Just that sort of thing happened to Jesus and His earthly parents, Mary and Joseph. When Jesus was twelve years old, they all went to Jerusalem to celebrate the Passover, just as they did every year. When the celebration was over, Mary and Joseph left for home, along with a big group of friends and relatives. They didn't realize Jesus wasn't with their group until they were well on their way.

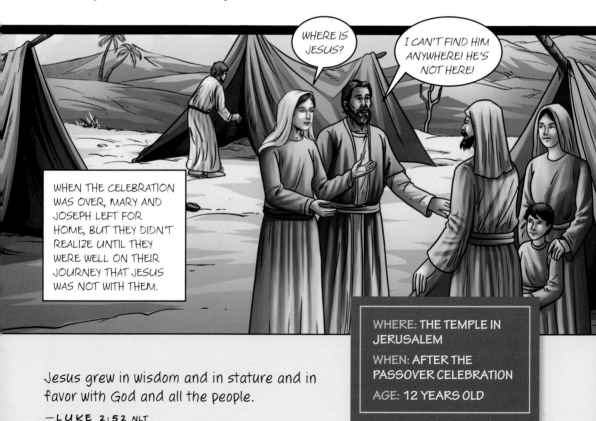

WHERE IS JESUS?

I CAN'T FIND HIM ANYWHERE! HE'S NOT HERE!

WHEN THE CELEBRATION WAS OVER, MARY AND JOSEPH LEFT FOR HOME, BUT THEY DIDN'T REALIZE UNTIL THEY WERE WELL ON THEIR JOURNEY THAT JESUS WAS NOT WITH THEM.

WHERE: THE TEMPLE IN JERUSALEM

WHEN: AFTER THE PASSOVER CELEBRATION

AGE: 12 YEARS OLD

Jesus grew in wisdom and in stature and in favor with God and all the people.

—LUKE 2:52 NLT

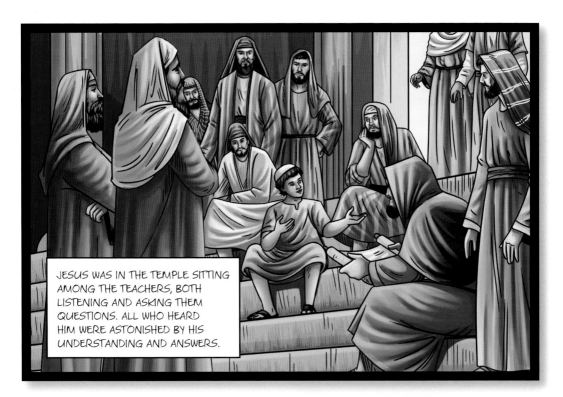

JESUS WAS IN THE TEMPLE SITTING AMONG THE TEACHERS, BOTH LISTENING AND ASKING THEM QUESTIONS. ALL WHO HEARD HIM WERE ASTONISHED BY HIS UNDERSTANDING AND ANSWERS.

After three terrifying days of searching through Jerusalem, they found Him. Where? In the temple courts, sitting with the teachers, listening, and asking questions. Mary and Joseph were amazed to find Him there, but they were also still upset. "Why have You done this?" Mary scolded. "Your father and I were worried."

But Jesus simply said, "Why were you searching? Didn't you know I would be in My Father's house?"

Jesus wasn't lost, and He wasn't worried. He was right where He needed to be—learning about God. Take time to learn from those around you who know God. Listen and ask questions. Just be sure your parents know where you are! ▶ LUKE 2

BE A HERO!

Be like Jesus and ask questions. Keep a journal of questions, and every now and then sit down with your parents, Bible teacher, or someone else who knows a lot about God. Ask your questions and listen to the answers. Then ask more questions! Heroes know there's always something new to learn about God.

🏃 **HERO TRAINING** Jesus is not the only person who the Bible says grew in "wisdom" and "stature" and "in favor with God." Look up Luke 1:80 and 1 Samuel 2:26 to find out who else these words describe. And check out the good news in Psalm 32:8. God will help you grow too!

A Voice in the Wilderness

John the Baptist—The Announcer

Have you ever been to a ballgame or a concert where an announcer told you what was coming next? Some announcers are pretty entertaining, but the real show is still to come. John the Baptist was a bit like an announcer. He told the people of Israel that Someone great was coming—Jesus!

MOTHER: ELIZABETH

FATHER: ZECHARIAH

COUSIN: JESUS

DID YOU KNOW? JOHN LIVED IN THE WILDERNESS, ATE WILD HONEY AND LOCUSTS, AND WORE CLOTHES MADE OF CAMEL HAIR.

He must become greater; I must become less.
—JOHN 3:30 NIV

AS JOHN PREACHED, CROWDS OF PEOPLE CAME TO HIM TO BE BAPTIZED IN THE JORDAN RIVER.

I BAPTIZE YOU WITH WATER.

John was Jesus' cousin. He first met Jesus when they were both still babies in their mothers' wombs. Years later, when John grew up, he began to preach. John wanted the whole world to know that the Savior was coming. "Change your hearts and lives," he warned. "The kingdom of heaven is coming soon!" He was talking about Jesus, the Savior.

Many people came to hear John speak, and many decided to change their hearts and lives. John baptized them as a sign of the change they were making. Some people thought John might be the Savior, but he told them, "I'm not Him. I'm not even worthy to carry His sandals!" Though many people came to hear John speak, he didn't care about impressing people or saying he was the best. John wanted everyone to know that Jesus was the greatest.

There will be times when you are the star of the show. Take that spotlight and shine it where it belongs—on Jesus. ▶MATTHEW 3; MARK 1; LUKE 3

🦸 BE A HERO!

You'll have opportunities to be the star of the show, and that's great. But be willing to let others shine too. For example, do you always decide what activities you and your friends will do? Do you always answer the questions in class and always take the lead? Let someone else be the star sometimes. Heroes let others shine.

🦸 HERO TRAINING Even though John preached to many people, he was humble. He knew that Jesus was greater than he was, and his job was to point people to Jesus. Look up Philippians 2:3 to see how you can be humble like John.

Baptized!

Jesus—The Son of God

I HAVE COME HERE TO BE BAPTIZED.

God gives us signs of change. When the sun rises, we know day is coming. When the sun sets, night is coming. There are signs for spring, summer, fall, and winter. God also gives us signs for changes in our lives. One of those signs is baptism.

John was often called John the Baptist because he baptized people. Baptism showed

MASTER, YOU SHOULD BE BAPTIZING ME!

IT IS WHAT GOD WANTS.

WHERE: THE JORDAN RIVER

AGE: 30 YEARS OLD

DID YOU KNOW? JESUS' BAPTISM IS USUALLY THOUGHT OF AS THE BEGINNING OF HIS MINISTRY.

Change your hearts and lives and be baptized, each one of you, in the name of Jesus Christ for the forgiveness of your sins. And you will receive the gift of the Holy Spirit.

—ACTS 2:38 NCV

that they had changed their hearts and lives, turned away from sin, and decided to follow God. "I baptize you with water," John told the people. "But there is One who will baptize you with the Holy Spirit." John was talking about Jesus.

John was preaching by the Jordan River when Jesus came to him. Jesus wanted John to baptize Him. "Why do you come to me to be baptized?" John asked. "I should be baptized by you!" But Jesus said it needed to be this way, so John obeyed.

As Jesus was coming up out of the water, the heavens opened, and God's Spirit came down on Jesus like a dove. A voice from heaven called out, "This is My Son. I love Him. I am very pleased with Him."

When we decide to change our lives and follow Jesus instead of the world, baptism is a part of that change in our lives. It shows the world that Jesus has washed away our sins and the Holy Spirit of God lives inside us. ▶ MATTHEW 3; MARK 1; LUKE 3

JOHN BAPTIZED JESUS IN THE JORDAN RIVER, AND THE HEAVENS OPENED UP. A VOICE FROM ABOVE SAID, "THIS IS MY BELOVED SON, IN WHOM I AM WELL PLEASED."

🏃 HERO TRAINING The New Testament has several stories about baptism. Read Acts 8:26–40 to discover the story of Philip and the Ethiopian. And check out Acts 9:1–19 for the baptism of Saul and the story of how he changed from hating Jesus to loving Him with all his heart.

🦸 BE A HERO!

Jesus never sinned, so there was no need to change His heart or life. There was no need to wash His sins away. He was baptized as an example for us. You, too, are an example. Make sure the way you live is a clear sign that you follow Jesus.

Standing on the Word of God

Jesus—The Tempted

Imagine this: You stop by your empty classroom after school to grab your lunchbox. And there—just sitting on the teacher's desk—is tomorrow's big test, with the answers in red. You know it's wrong, but no one would know if you took a quick peek, right? That is temptation. And Jesus completely understands.

Shortly after Jesus was baptized, the Spirit led Him into the wilderness. He stayed there for forty days and forty nights, not eating a thing. That's when Satan showed up.

"If you are the Son of God, tell these rocks to become bread," Satan told Jesus. Of course,

JESUS STAYED IN THE WILDERNESS FOR 40 DAYS AND 40 NIGHTS.

HE ATE NOTHING DURING THOSE DAYS. HE WAS HUNGRY.

WHERE: THE DESERT OF JUDEA, WHICH LIES BETWEEN JERUSALEM AND THE DEAD SEA

WHEN: SHORTLY AFTER JESUS' BAPTISM

For our high priest is able to understand our weaknesses. He was tempted in every way that we are, but he did not sin.

—HEBREWS 4:15 ICB

Jesus really was the Son of God. And He was hungry! It would've been so easy to turn those rocks into bread. But Jesus knew He shouldn't use His holy power for Himself. He answered Satan with God's own Word: "A person lives not on bread alone but by everything God says."

Jesus responded the same way when Satan offered Him all the world's riches if Jesus would worship him. Jesus quoted God's Word: "Worship the Lord and serve Him only." Then Satan took Jesus to the top of the temple. He tempted Jesus to test God's faithfulness by jumping off, but Jesus again used God's Word to defeat the evil one. "Don't put God to the test," He said. After that, Satan went away, but only for a time.

BE A HERO!

Turning away from temptation can be tough, but it's easier with a friend. If your friend is tempted to do the wrong thing, pray for him or her. Encourage one another to do what's right. Two are better than one when it comes to fighting temptation. And when you've got God on your side, you're undefeatable.

All throughout His life, Jesus was tempted—in every way you are. But He never gave in. He'll help you stand strong and do what's right too. ▶*Matthew 4; Mark 1; Luke 4*

HERO TRAINING Jesus used one weapon to defeat Satan, and it's a weapon that you can use too: God's Word. Read Hebrews 4:12 and Ephesians 6:17 to see how God's Word is your sword to defeat the evil one.

It's Hard to Go Home

Jesus—The Hometown Prophet

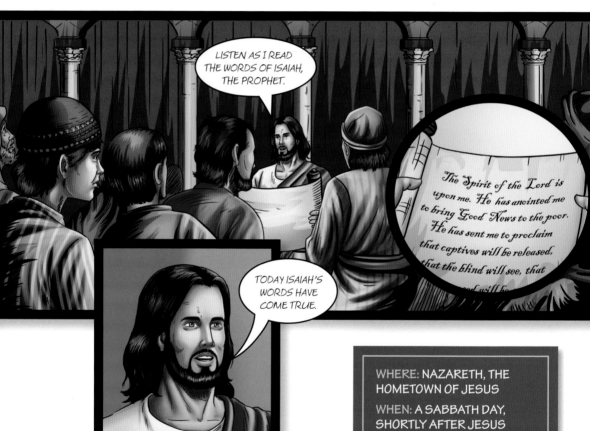

LISTEN AS I READ THE WORDS OF ISAIAH, THE PROPHET.

The Spirit of the Lord is upon me. He has anointed me to bring Good News to the poor. He has sent me to proclaim that captives will be released, that the blind will see, that

TODAY ISAIAH'S WORDS HAVE COME TRUE.

WHERE: NAZARETH, THE HOMETOWN OF JESUS

WHEN: A SABBATH DAY, SHORTLY AFTER JESUS BEGAN HIS MINISTRY

KEY TERM: MESSIAH: "ANOINTED ONE"; ANOTHER WORD FOR THE PROMISED SAVIOR, JESUS

DID YOU KNOW? ON THIS SABBATH DAY, JESUS READ FROM ISAIAH 58 AND 61.

"If the world hates you, remember that it hated me first. If you belonged to the world, then it would love you as it loves its own. But I have chosen you out of the world. So you don't belong to it. That is why the world hates you."

—JOHN 15:18–19 ICB

eing the last one picked when choosing teams for a game. Being the only one not invited to the party. Having no one to sit with at lunch. Being left out or rejected is no fun. It hurts and nobody likes it. But everyone gets rejected at some point in their lives. Even Jesus.

Not long after Jesus was tempted by Satan, He returned to Nazareth, where He grew up. On the Sabbath day, He went to the synagogue, just as He always did. That day Jesus stood up to read from the book of Isaiah. The passage talked about the coming Messiah. When Jesus finished reading, He said, "These words have now come true." He was the Messiah!

"Isn't this Joseph's son?" the people asked. How could He be the Messiah? They became so angry, they led Jesus to the top of a cliff and were about to throw Him off. (Now that's rejection!) But Jesus calmly walked through the crowd and went on His way.

THE PEOPLE WERE SO ENRAGED WHEN THEY HEARD JESUS SPEAK THESE WORDS THAT THEY FORCED HIM FROM THE TEMPLE AND INTO THE STREET.

There will be times when you are left out, made fun of, and rejected. Sometimes it will even be because you follow Jesus. Just keep doing the things you know are right. Jesus understands, and He'll help you get through—just as He got through that angry crowd. ▶ *LUKE 4*

HERO TRAINING The people of Nazareth didn't want to hear what Jesus had to say. Perhaps they knew that accepting Him as Savior would require them to change the way they lived. When you share Jesus' message, it forces people to think about the way they live—and they might not like that! But look at what Jesus promises in Luke 6:22–23.

BE A HERO!

Think of a time you were left out or rejected. How did it feel? Pretty lousy, right? Make sure no one around you ever feels like that. See someone eating alone? Join him. That kid who's always picked last for the team? Pick her first! Make everyone feel welcome around you.

"Follow Me"

The Disciples—Called by Jesus

SIMON LEFT HIS NETS BEHIND THAT VERY DAY TO FOLLOW JESUS, AND SO TOO DID HIS FELLOW FISHERMEN ANDREW, JAMES, AND JOHN.

LORD, YOU SHOULD LEAVE ME, FOR I AM A SINFUL MAN!

DON'T BE AFRAID. FROM THIS DAY ON, YOU WILL BE CALLED PETER. YOU WILL BE A FISHER OF MEN.

WHO: SIMON PETER, ANDREW, JAMES, JOHN, PHILIP, NATHANAEL (OR BARTHOLOMEW), THOMAS, MATTHEW, JAMES THE LESSER, THADDAEUS (OR JUDE), SIMON THE ZEALOT, AND JUDAS ISCARIOT

JOBS: THE GROUP OF DISCIPLES INCLUDED FISHERMEN, A TAX COLLECTOR, AND A REBEL AGAINST ROME

They left everything and followed Jesus.
—LUKE 5:11 ICB

When you hear the word *call*, you probably think of a phone. But in the Bible, *call* is the word used when Jesus asked someone to follow Him or do something for Him. And similar to picking up a ringing phone, when Jesus called the disciples, they answered!

The first person to answer Jesus' call was a fisherman named Simon. Jesus had climbed into Simon's boat near the Sea of Galilee to speak to a crowd. When Jesus finished speaking, He said to Simon, "Sail to the deepest part of the lake and cast out your nets."

Now, Simon was a professional fisherman. He had fished all night long and hadn't caught a single fish. But he did as Jesus said. Simon caught so many fish that the boat began to sink!

Simon was frightened, but Jesus said, "Don't be afraid! From this day on, you'll be called Peter, and you'll be a fisher of men." Simon (now Peter), along with his fishing partners Andrew, James, and John, left their boats and followed Jesus.

Another day Jesus came upon Matthew, a tax collector. Jesus said. "Leave everything behind, and follow Me." And Matthew did. Then several others followed Jesus too! The disciples were just ordinary people, but they chose to leave behind the things of this world and follow Jesus.

That's what Jesus is calling you to do too. Leave behind the things the world says are important. Put following Jesus first in your life. ▶ *Matthew 4, 9–10; Mark 1, 3; Luke 5–6*

🏃 HERO TRAINING There is one never-fail way for people to know that you are a follower of Jesus. Find out what it is in John 13:34–35.

Living Water

The Samaritan Woman—Who Spoke to Jesus

"Whoever drinks the water I give will never be thirsty again. The water I give will become a spring of water flowing inside him. It will give him eternal life."

—JOHN 4:14 ICB

WHERE: JACOB'S WELL IN SAMARIA, WHICH IS STILL IN ISRAEL TODAY

KEY TERM: SAMARITANS: A PEOPLE GROUP WHO WERE LOOKED DOWN ON BY THE JEWS

magine a hot, sunny day. You've been playing outside for hours, and your throat is so dry it almost hurts. How wonderful would a drink of water be? Not just a tiny sip but a tall glass brimming with cool, clear water.

Jesus once compared Himself to water. As He walked through Samaria one day, He stopped to rest near Jacob's well. When a woman came to draw water, Jesus asked her for a drink. The woman was surprised! Jewish men never talked to Samaritan women.

Then Jesus surprised her yet again. He said, "If you knew who I was, you would have asked me, and I would have given you living water." *How could this man give me water?* the woman wondered. *He doesn't even have a bucket.* Jesus then said, "Everyone who drinks from this well will be thirsty again. But those who drink from the water I give them will never be thirsty again. I give the water of eternal life."

As they talked, the woman realized this was the Messiah. He knew everything about her! She left her water jar and ran to tell everyone about Jesus. Jesus stayed and taught for two days in that town, and many people came to believe in Him.

Jesus offered the people more than simple water that would quench their bodies' thirst. He offered them the living water of His Spirit that would satisfy the thirst in their souls. Jesus offers that same living water to you. Just open His Word, take a deep drink, and believe.

▶ JOHN 4

🗡 **HERO TRAINING** Jesus not only promised to quench our thirst; He also promised to satisfy our hunger. Look up John 6:35. What does Jesus call Himself?

THE WOMAN LEFT HER WATER JAR AND WENT INTO TOWN TO TELL PEOPLE ABOUT JESUS.

COME SEE THE PROPHET I HAVE MET. I BELIEVE HE IS THE MESSIAH!

JESUS STAYED IN THE TOWN FOR TWO DAYS, AND MANY PEOPLE CAME TO BELIEVE IN HIM.

Amazing Faith

The Centurion—A Soldier of Faith

WHERE: CAPERNAUM, A SMALL TOWN NEAR NAZARETH

KEY TERM: CENTURION: A ROMAN MILITARY OFFICER IN CHARGE OF 100 SOLDIERS

The officer answered, "Lord, I am not worthy for you to come into my house. You only need to command it, and my servant will be healed."
—MATTHEW 8:8 NCV

What makes you stop and say, "Wow!"? Is it the stars or the sunrise? Perhaps it's the gizmos inside a computer or the way an airplane takes flight. Did you know that Jesus was sometimes amazed? Jesus was also fully human, and He experienced every emotion that we do. So what amazed the Son of God?

Jesus had just arrived in Capernaum when a Roman centurion came to Him. The soldier bowed before Jesus. Then he told Jesus about his servant who was terribly ill. Jesus offered to come to the man's house and heal the servant. But the centurion said, "Lord, I am not worthy for you to come into my house. You need only command it, and my servant will be healed." He explained that he was a man in charge of other soldiers, and when he commanded something to be done, it was done.

Jesus was amazed by the man's faith. "Go home," He said. "Your servant will be healed just as you believed he would." And he was.

The centurion trusted that Jesus was able to do whatever He said He would do. And that's a pretty good definition of faith for us too. ▶ MATTHEW 8; LUKE 7

BE A HERO!

Military workers are heroes who defend our nation and keep us safe. When you see a soldier, step up and say, "Thank you for your service!" Then ask if you can pray for him or her.

🏃 HERO TRAINING What is faith? Read the explanation in Hebrews 11:1 and 1 Peter 1:8. What are some things you can't see but have faith they are real?

Childlike Faith

Jesus—Who Welcomed Children

"I tell you the truth. You must accept the kingdom of God as a little child accepts things, or you will never enter it."

—MARK 10:15 ICB

WHERE: JUDEA

KEY TERM: KINGDOM OF GOD: THE RULE OF GOD; ALSO CALLED THE KINGDOM OF HEAVEN

Imagine you're going swimming with your dad. He's in the deep end, and you're up on the diving board, trying to find enough courage to jump in. Then your dad says, "Don't worry! I'll catch you!" So you grin and jump right in. You know he'll catch you, just as he said. That's a childlike faith. And Jesus wishes a whole lot more grown-ups had it.

In fact, Jesus once told His disciples they needed a childlike faith in God. It happened one day when Jesus was teaching. You see, everywhere He went, people brought their children to Him so that He could pray for them. (After all, who wouldn't want a hug and a prayer from Jesus?) But this time some of His disciples told the people to leave Jesus alone. He was too busy to talk to children, they said.

When Jesus heard this, it made him angry. "Let the little children come to Me," He said. "Don't stop them. I tell you the truth—you must accept the kingdom of God as a little child accepts things, or you will never enter it." Then Jesus scooped the children up in His arms and blessed them.

So what is a childlike faith? It's knowing you can't do everything on your own. It's not being afraid to run to Jesus for help. And it's trusting Him completely, knowing He'll always catch you. No matter how grown-up you get to be, hold on to your childlike faith.

▶ MATTHEW 19; MARK 10; LUKE 18

🏃 HERO TRAINING Like a child jumping into a father's arms, you sometimes need to jump out in faith. Obey God and trust Him to catch you. Read Psalm 121 to discover some of the ways God watches over you.

BE A HERO!

When Jesus scooped up those children, they must have been given the world's best hug! Your hugs are pretty powerful too. They can say, "I love you," "I'm sorry," and "I'm here for you." Be a hero and hug a friend in need today!

Joy in Heaven

The Faithful Shepherd—Who Lost and Found

What do you do if you lose your allowance? Do you say, "Oh well. It would have been nice to have that"? Of course not! You search high and low for it. You ask your mom and dad if they've seen it. And when you finally find it, you're so happy you just have to shout, "Woohoo!" That's exactly what the angels in heaven do when a lost person is found by God.

Jesus came to seek and to save the lost. So while He was on earth, He spent a lot of time with sinners and tax collectors, people who often made the wrong choices. The

JESUS HEARD THE PHARISEES TALKING ABOUT HIM. JESUS ASKED WHO AMONG THEM WOULD NOT LEAVE 99 SHEEP IN THE FIELD TO FIND THE ONE SHEEP THAT WAS LOST.

ONCE THE SHEEP WAS FOUND, JESUS SAID, WHO WOULD NOT CALL HIS FRIENDS TO CELEBRATE AND SAY, "I HAVE FOUND MY LOST SHEEP"?

WHO: JESUS AND THE PHARISEES (A RELIGIOUS GROUP KNOWN FOR STRICTLY FOLLOWING GOD'S LAWS BUT NOT ALWAYS HAVING A RELATIONSHIP WITH GOD)

KEY TERM: PARABLE: AN EARTHLY STORY WITH A DEEPER, HEAVENLY MEANING

"There is more joy in heaven over one lost sinner who repents and returns to God than over ninety-nine others who are righteous and haven't strayed away!"
—LUKE 15:7 NLT

Pharisees and teachers of the law didn't like that. They thought Jesus shouldn't be with those kinds of people.

To explain His actions, Jesus told this parable: "Imagine you have a hundred sheep, and one of them goes missing. Wouldn't you leave the ninety-nine to go and look for it? When you find it, wouldn't you joyfully carry it home? And wouldn't you call your friends and neighbors together and say, 'Rejoice with me! I have found my lost sheep!'?" Then Jesus added, "There is more joy in heaven over one sinner who repents and returns to God than over ninety-nine righteous people who didn't stray away!"

BE A HERO!

A shepherd isn't just the boss of the sheep. A shepherd guides, protects, and cares for the sheep. Think about those younger kids who look up to you: a brother or sister, cousins, or someone at church. How can you be a shepherd to them?

When you lose something, you don't let it stay lost. You search for it! In the same way, God searches for lost people. And He keeps searching until He brings them home. That's when the heavenly celebration begins! ▶ MATTHEW 18; LUKE 15

✗ **HERO TRAINING** Read John 10:11–15. What does Jesus do for His sheep? Now look up Isaiah 40:11. What does this tell you about the Shepherd's love for you?

To the Rescue!

The Good Samaritan—An Unexpected Hero

Have you ever tried to get out of something you didn't want to do? Maybe it was your turn to take out the trash. You know that means *all* the trash—from the kitchen, the bedrooms, the office. But you still ask your parents *which* trash. Because you don't want to do any more work than you have to.

That's exactly what a teacher of the law was doing. Jesus had just told him to love his neighbor as himself. But there were some people this man didn't really want to love. So he asked Jesus, "Who is my neighbor?"

Jesus answered him by telling a parable: "A man was traveling from Jerusalem to Jericho.

WHO: A PRIEST (A WORSHIP LEADER OF ISRAEL), A LEVITE (A TEMPLE WORKER), AND A SAMARITAN

WHERE: ON THE ROAD FROM JERUSALEM TO JERICHO

"Love your neighbor as yourself."
—LUKE 10:27 NIV

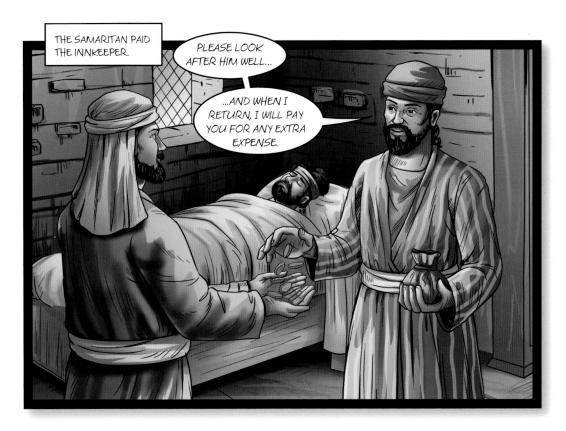

Suddenly, a group of robbers attacked him. They beat him, stole his clothes, and left him to die. A priest saw the hurt traveler but didn't stop. A Levite also saw him and kept walking. But a Samaritan (who was hated by the Jews) did stop. That wasn't all, either. He bandaged the man's wounds, put the traveler on his own donkey, and took him to an inn. There, the Samaritan paid the innkeeper to look after the man."

Then Jesus asked, "Which of these three men was a good neighbor?" Of course, it was the Samaritan!

Even though the priest and Levite were supposed to be God's workers, it was the Samaritan who went way out of his way to help. When you see people in need, don't ignore them or wish them good luck—go out of your way to help! ▶ *LUKE 10*

🏃 **HERO TRAINING** Read James 2:14–17. Why do you think faith without works (that is, saying you love God but not helping His people) is dead faith?

🦸 BE A HERO!

Acts 10:38 tells us that Jesus went about doing good things everywhere He went. Here's a hero's challenge: Be like Jesus. Whether it's at school, in the park, or simply at the dinner table, do something good everywhere you go!

Coming Home

The Father—Who Wouldn't Give Up

Some people see God as a heavenly grandfather who doesn't do much in our lives. Others see Him as an angry authority figure who is just waiting for us to mess up so He can zap us. But neither of those ideas is actually true.

Jesus wanted people to understand what God was really like, so He told a parable: A man had two sons. The younger son asked his father for his share of the father's money. The father gave it to him, and the son left town and quickly spent everything. By the time a

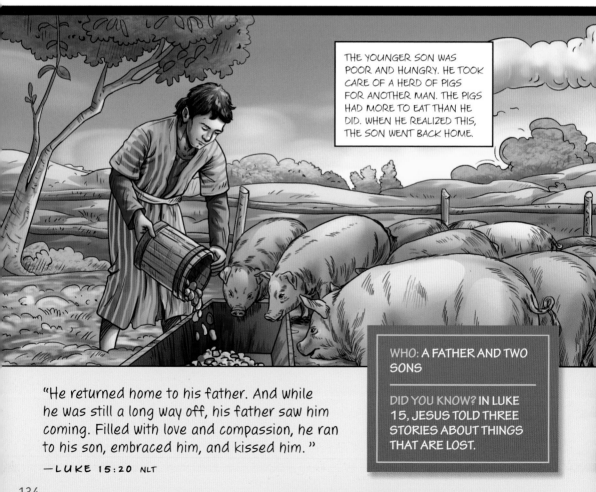

THE YOUNGER SON WAS POOR AND HUNGRY. HE TOOK CARE OF A HERD OF PIGS FOR ANOTHER MAN. THE PIGS HAD MORE TO EAT THAN HE DID. WHEN HE REALIZED THIS, THE SON WENT BACK HOME.

"He returned home to his father. And while he was still a long way off, his father saw him coming. Filled with love and compassion, he ran to his son, embraced him, and kissed him."

—LUKE 15:20 NLT

WHO: A FATHER AND TWO SONS

DID YOU KNOW? IN LUKE 15, JESUS TOLD THREE STORIES ABOUT THINGS THAT ARE LOST.

famine hit and food was hard to find, the son was poor. He ended up feeding pigs, wishing he could eat the animals' food.

That's when he realized that even his father's servants were better off than he was. So he decided to go home. Though he knew he wasn't worthy of being a son anymore, he hoped his father would let him be a servant. At least he wouldn't be hungry!

As the son was walking up the road home, his father saw him. The father ran to meet his lost son. And he wasn't angry at all! In fact, he hugged him and threw him a party.

God is like that father. He's always ready to welcome His children home. There is no anger. There is only great joy. No matter what you've done or said, no matter how badly you've messed up, God is always ready to welcome you home! ▶ *LUKE 15*

🏃 **HERO TRAINING** There will come a time when you're in the position of the younger son. You'll sin and you'll need to go back to the Father. Tell Him you're sorry (that's called confession), and ask Him to forgive you. He always will! That's the promise of 1 John 1:9. Check it out.

🦹 BE A HERO!

When the father threw a party for his younger son, the older son was mad. After all, he had done all the right things, and no one had thrown him a party. Don't let that be your attitude when a sinner comes to Jesus. Instead, join the party! Heroes celebrate with God when a sinner comes home.

THIS SON OF MINE WAS DEAD AND IS ALIVE AGAIN; HE WAS LOST AND IS FOUND.

Through the Roof

A Paralyzed Man—Brought to Jesus

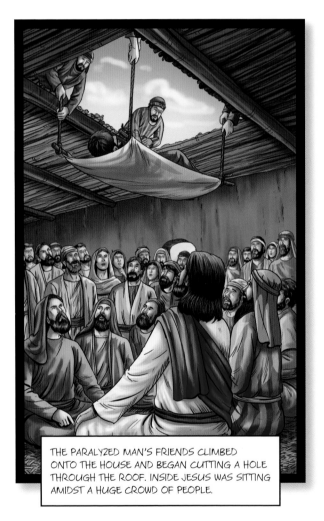

THE PARALYZED MAN'S FRIENDS CLIMBED ONTO THE HOUSE AND BEGAN CUTTING A HOLE THROUGH THE ROOF. INSIDE JESUS WAS SITTING AMIDST A HUGE CROWD OF PEOPLE.

What would you do to see Jesus face-to-face? Would you take a car, a boat, a plane, or a train to travel to Him? Would you wait in line for days? Would you cut a hole through a roof? Wait . . . that last one's a bit crazy, isn't it? But that's exactly what four friends did.

You see, they heard that Jesus was teaching in a house in Capernaum. And they just had to see Him—not for themselves but for their friend. He couldn't walk, and Jesus was his only hope. So they put the man on a mat and carried him to the house. But people were everywhere. They couldn't get anywhere near Jesus.

Then one of them had a crazy idea. They climbed up on the roof, cut a

WHO: A PARALYZED MAN AND FOUR FRIENDS

WHERE: CAPERNAUM

DID YOU KNOW? IN BIBLE TIMES, A TYPICAL HOUSE HAD A FLAT ROOF MADE OF WOOD AND BRANCHES THAT WAS COVERED WITH CLAY.

Pray for all people. Ask God for the things people need, and be thankful to him.
—1 TIMOTHY 2:1 ICB

hole in it, and lowered their friend right down in front of Jesus! Can you imagine what the people inside must have thought?

Jesus didn't seem to mind, though. He saw the friends' faith and said to the paralyzed man, "Your sins are forgiven."

Among the crowd were some teachers of the law. *Who does He think He is?* they thought. Only God can forgive sins!

Jesus knew their thoughts and said, "Which is easier: to say, 'Your sins are forgiven' or to say 'Rise, pick up your mat, and walk'?" Then He told the man to do just that, and the man did!

Those four men were determined to help their friend get to Jesus, and it changed his life. What can you do to help your friends get to Jesus so He can change their lives too?

▶ *MARK 2; LUKE 5*

🏃 **HERO TRAINING** Read John 15:15. What does Jesus call those who follow Him? His friends! And just as you can carry your friends to God in prayer, Jesus carries you to God in prayer. Read Romans 8:34 and check out this beautiful promise for yourself!

🏃 **BE A HERO!**

When friends are hurting or in trouble, sometimes you can help them yourself, and sometimes you can't. But God can *always* help. Carry your friends to Him in prayer. Talk to God about their hurts and troubles. Ask Him to help—and to show you how to help too.

WHEN JESUS FORGAVE THE PARALYZED MAN'S SINS, THE TEACHERS OF THE LAW WERE ANGRY. JESUS KNEW IN HIS MIND WHAT THE MEN WERE THINKING.

WHICH IS EASIER— TO SAY TO THIS MAN, "YOUR SINS ARE FORGIVEN"?

OR TO SAY, "RISE, PICK UP YOUR MAT, AND WALK"?

THE SON OF MAN HAS AUTHORITY ON EARTH TO FORGIVE SINS.

GET UP, PICK UP YOUR MAT, AND GO HOME.

THE MAN DID AS JESUS COMMANDED. EVERYONE WHO WITNESSED THE EVENT WAS AMAZED, FOR THEY HAD NEVER SEEN ANYTHING LIKE THIS BEFORE.

Even the Wind and Waves

Jesus—Who Calms Storms

Storms can be big and noisy with howling wind and pounding rain. And perhaps the most frightening part is that you have no control over them! If your music is too loud, you can turn it down. If your bike is going too fast, you can put on the brakes. But there's nothing you can do about a storm.

The disciples discovered that there is someone who can control a storm, though: Jesus. It all happened when they were out on the Sea of Galilee. Jesus and His disciples were sailing to the other side when a terrible storm came up. Waves crashed over the sides of the boat and threatened to sink it. The disciples were terrified!

But Jesus wasn't worried. In fact, He was sound asleep! The disciples woke Him up. "Don't You care if we drown?" they asked.

Jesus calmly stood and said into the night, "Quiet! Be still!" The wind and the waves obeyed

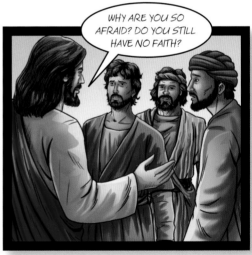

WHO: JESUS AND HIS DISCIPLES

WHERE: IN A BOAT ON THE SEA OF GALILEE

This hope is a strong and trustworthy anchor for our souls.
—HEBREWS 6:19 NLT

Him. Then Jesus turned to His disciples and asked, "Why were you so afraid? Where is your faith?"

The disciples looked at each other. "Who is this?" they asked. "Even the wind and the waves obey Him."

Storms are no match for the power of Jesus, not the storms of nature and not the storms of troubles that come into our lives. When waves of problems are tossing you all around, remember that Jesus is more powerful than any storm—and He is in control!

▶ MATTHEW 8; MARK 4; LUKE 8

BE A HERO!

Heroes are prepared when storms hit. Put together an emergency storm kit for your family. Include things like flashlights, a weather radio, a deck of cards, and a Bible. (You can get more ideas at www.ready.gov /build-a-kit.) Remember that Jesus is always with you through any kind of storm.

🏃 HERO TRAINING Even before Jesus stopped the storm, He was right there with them in the boat. Sometimes Jesus will stop your storms. Sometimes He won't. But look at the promise of Psalm 46:1–2. He's always right there with you.

Food for a Crowd

A Boy—Who Gave What He Had

THIS BOY HAS FIVE BARLEY LOAVES AND TWO FISH. BUT I DON'T KNOW HOW MUCH USE THEY WILL BE WITH SO MANY PEOPLE!

Think about what you had for lunch today. Maybe it was a sandwich and some chips or perhaps a slice of pizza and some fruit. Did you have enough to share with a friend? What about five friends? Or ten? How about five thousand friends or more? Impossible, right?

One boy found out that the impossible was possible when he gave his lunch to Jesus. It wasn't much of a lunch. Just five little loaves of bread and a couple small fish. But Jesus turned it into a feast!

My God will use his wonderful riches in Christ Jesus to give you everything you need.
—PHILIPPIANS 4:19 ICB

WHO: 5,000 MEN, PLUS WOMEN AND CHILDREN

WHERE: NEAR THE SEA OF GALILEE

After a long day of teaching, thousands of people were gathered to hear Jesus. The sun was starting to set, and the people were hungry. Jesus asked Philip, "Where can we buy bread for these people?" Philip was astounded! They didn't have enough money for that!

Then Andrew brought a boy to Jesus. That boy gave Jesus his lunch. Jesus gave thanks for the food, and the disciples began giving it to the people. Everyone had more than enough to eat. The disciples even picked up twelve baskets of leftovers.

That boy gave Jesus what he had. Jesus used it to do something amazing. And He'll do the same for you. Give what you have to Jesus—your time, your talents, your possessions. He'll use what you give to do something amazing!

▶ *MATTHEW 14; MARK 6; LUKE 9; JOHN 6*

🏃 HERO TRAINING In Luke 18:27, Jesus said that what's impossible for people is possible for God. What are some of your favorite impossible things from the Bible? Here's a funny one to get you started: Matthew 17:24–27.

🦸 BE A HERO!

Share a lunch with one of your heroes—a grandparent, teacher, firefighter, or anyone you look up to. But don't just give your lunch and walk away. Sit down, share the meal, have a conversation. Find out how you can pray for him or her.

THE DISCIPLES KEPT ON HANDING OUT FOOD. THERE WAS ALWAYS MORE BREAD AND FISH TO REFILL THE BASKETS. WHEN EVERYONE HAD EATEN, JESUS' DISCIPLES COLLECTED WHAT WAS LEFT. THE BITS AND PIECES OF FOOD FILLED 12 BASKETS.

Walking on Water

Peter—Who Stepped Out of the Boat

JOBS: FISHERMAN, DISCIPLE, AND CHURCH LEADER

BROTHER: ANDREW

WHERE: THE SEA OF GALILEE

WHEN: IN THE MIDDLE OF THE NIGHT, AFTER JESUS FED THE 5,000

Let us look only to Jesus. He is the one who began our faith, and he makes our faith perfect.

—HEBREWS 12:2 ICB

When you're riding a bicycle, it's important to keep your eyes fixed on where you're going. If you look to the left, pretty soon you'll be heading left. Look to the right, and you'll head right. That's a lesson Peter learned the hard way—not on a bike, but in the middle of a storm on the Sea of Galilee.

After Jesus fed the five thousand, He told the disciples to sail across the sea. Jesus then went up on the mountain alone to pray. It was the middle of the night, and the disciples had rowed far out when a terrible storm hit.

As they were battling the waves, they saw a figure walking on the water toward them. At first, they thought it was a ghost. But then Jesus called out, "Take courage! It is I. Don't be afraid."

Peter looked at Him and said, "If it's You, Lord, tell me to come to You on the water." Jesus did, and Peter stepped out of the boat. He walked on the water toward Jesus!

But then Peter looked at the wind and the waves, and he became afraid. Starting to sink, Peter cried out, "Lord, save me!" And Jesus did.

Peter was safe as long as he kept his eyes on Jesus. But when the storm grabbed his attention, he started to sink. Don't let life's troubles pull you away from Jesus. Always keep your eyes on Him. ▶MATTHEW 14; MARK 6; LUKE 6

BE A HERO!

Some people scold Peter for taking his eyes off Jesus. But think about this: Peter was the only disciple brave enough to get out of the boat. There will be times when you try to do something for Jesus and it doesn't go right. Don't beat yourself up. Talk to Jesus about it. And remember, He's glad you were brave enough to "step out of the boat."

🏃 **HERO TRAINING** Jesus was dealing with some storms in His life: John the Baptist had been beheaded. And those five thousand people He had fed wanted to make Him a king. So what did Jesus do? Find out in Matthew 14:23. When your life is stormy, do what Jesus did!

LORD, IF IT IS YOU, COMMAND ME TO COME TO YOU ON THE WATER.

COME TO ME, PETER!

BUT WHEN HE LOOKED AROUND HIM AT THE WIND AND THE WAVES, HE BECAME AFRAID AND BEGAN TO SINK. HE CRIED OUT TO JESUS TO SAVE HIM.

YOU OF LITTLE FAITH, WHY DID YOU DOUBT?

ONCE JESUS AND PETER WERE BOTH IN THE BOAT, THE WIND CALMED DOWN. THOSE IN THE BOAT NOW KNEW HE WAS TRULY THE SON OF GOD, AND THEY WORSHIPPED HIM.

"Help Me Believe!"

A Father—Who Asked for Help Believing

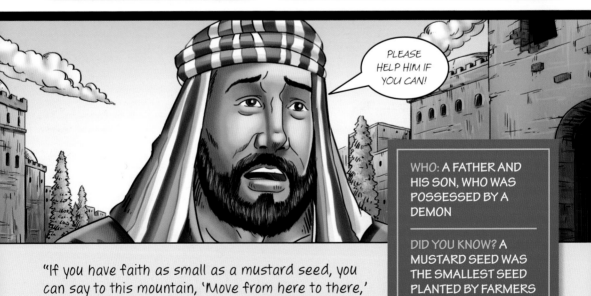

"If you have faith as small as a mustard seed, you can say to this mountain, 'Move from here to there,' and it will move. Nothing will be impossible for you."

—MATTHEW 17:20 NIV

WHO: A FATHER AND HIS SON, WHO WAS POSSESSED BY A DEMON

DID YOU KNOW? A MUSTARD SEED WAS THE SMALLEST SEED PLANTED BY FARMERS IN BIBLE TIMES.

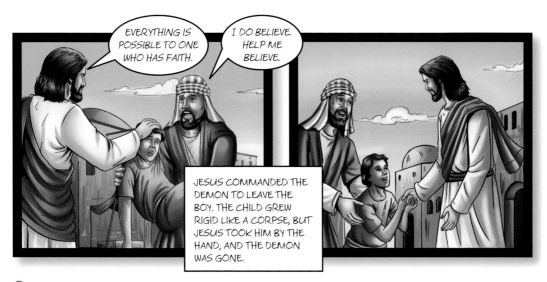

Let's be honest, sometimes it's hard to believe. When bad days stack up like building blocks, when plans fall apart, when there is sickness or sadness, it can be hard to believe God will work everything out. God doesn't ask for our faith to be perfect. He just asks for us to bring our faith to Him—and let Him make it perfect.

That's what one father did. His son was sick, but it was no ordinary sickness. It was caused by a demon. The father had taken his son to Jesus' disciples, but they couldn't help. So the father took his child to Jesus. "Please, help him if you can!" the father begged.

Jesus answered, "Everything is possible for one who believes."

That father desperately wanted to believe Jesus could help. But he still had doubts. After all, Jesus' disciples hadn't been able to help. So he said, "I do believe! Help me believe!" He knew his faith wasn't perfect, so he asked Jesus for help.

Jesus cast out the demon, and the son was healed. Later, Jesus told His disciples that if they would have faith the size of a tiny mustard seed, they would be able to move a mountain.

When everything is going your way, it's easy to have mountain-size faith. But when everything is going wrong, hold on to your faith. Even if it's as tiny as a mustard seed, give it to Jesus. He'll help you move those mountains. ▶ MATTHEW 17; MARK 9; LUKE 9

🏃 HERO TRAINING This story isn't the only time Jesus talked about a mustard seed. Read the parable of the mustard seed in Matthew 13:31–32. Here the mustard seed represents the kingdom of heaven. How does Jesus say it will grow?

🏃 BE A HERO!

Jesus is able to take a tiny seed of your faith and grow it into something strong enough to move mountains. Watch the wonder of a seed for yourself. Plant some vegetable seeds in your own garden or in a community garden. Give the food you grow to someone in need.

A Thankful Heart

The Leper—Who Turned Back

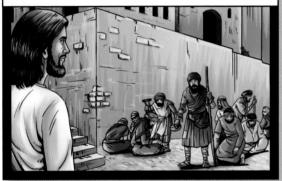

JESUS WAS ON HIS WAY TO JERUSALEM WHEN HE ENCOUNTERED A GROUP OF 10 LEPERS IN THE STREET.

t's probably happened to you. You were given the most amazing gift—the one you'd been waiting and hoping for. Maybe it was a new bike, a video game, or an art kit. You were so excited to start using it that you completely forgot to say thank you.

Perhaps that's what happened to some guys who received an amazing gift from Jesus. You see, as Jesus was on His way to Jerusalem, He met ten

JESUS, MASTER, HAVE **MERCY** ON US!

MAKE US **CLEAN!**

GO, SHOW YOURSELVES TO THE **PRIESTS**.

WHO: 10 MEN WITH LEPROSY

WHERE: A VILLAGE BETWEEN SAMARIA AND GALILEE

KEY TERM: LEPROSY: A CONTAGIOUS SKIN DISEASE; IN BIBLE TIMES PEOPLE WITH LEPROSY LIVED APART FROM EVERYONE ELSE

Thanks be to God for his gift that is too wonderful to explain.
—2 CORINTHIANS 9:15 ICB

lepers. In Jewish culture, leprosy made a person "unclean," which meant that lepers had to live apart from everyone else. They lost their families, jobs, everything. No one would touch a leper for fear of catching the disease. The ten lepers called out to Jesus, "Have mercy on us! Make us clean!"

Jesus said, "Go, show yourselves to the priests." Off the lepers ran, and as they went, they were healed!

One of the men, seeing that he was healed, came back. He threw himself at Jesus' feet and thanked Him. Jesus asked, "Weren't all ten cleansed? Are you the only one who has returned to give thanks? Stand up. Your faith has saved you."

👤 BE A HERO!

When friends or family members are in the hospital, they may feel separated from the rest of the world. Bring a bit of comfort to their day by gathering some packaged snacks in a basket. Leave the basket in a hospital waiting room along with a note saying that Jesus loves them!

Ten men were healed, but only one turned back to thank Jesus. It's easy to get caught up in the moment, to be so excited over a gift or an answered prayer that you forget to say thanks. If you happen to forget, run back to Jesus in prayer and thank Him for His amazing gifts!

▶ *LUKE 17*

🏃 **HERO TRAINING** You've probably heard the words "have a thankful heart." But what does that mean? It's more than just being grateful for a gift. It's being grateful for the One who gave you the gift. Jesus has given us the best gift of all—salvation (Ephesians 2:8–9). Thank Him today!

"I Want to See!"

Bartimaeus—The Blind Beggar

When you are sick or someone you love is sick, you pray. Because even though doctors and nurses can help (and your parents too), you know God is the One who does the healing.

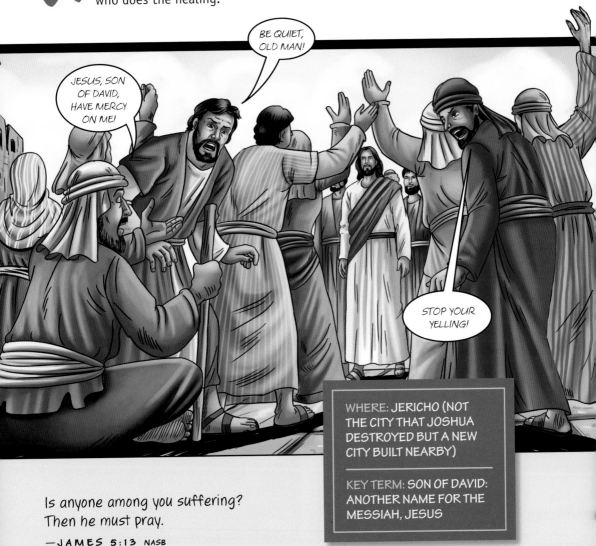

WHERE: JERICHO (NOT THE CITY THAT JOSHUA DESTROYED BUT A NEW CITY BUILT NEARBY)

KEY TERM: SON OF DAVID: ANOTHER NAME FOR THE MESSIAH, JESUS

Is anyone among you suffering? Then he must pray.
—JAMES 5:13 NASB

Bartimaeus knew there was no one who could heal him. Bartimaeus was blind, and no one could help him to see. That's why he sat by the road one day, begging for food and coins as he always did. And he didn't have much hope that this day would be any different from all the rest.

Then he heard the cheers of a crowd. Someone was coming. "It's Jesus," the people told him. This was it! This was his chance. Bartimaeus called out, "Jesus, Son of David, have mercy on me!" The people shushed him, but Bartimaeus just shouted louder.

Jesus heard him and said, "Bring that man to Me." Bartimaeus jumped up, threw off his cloak, and hurried to Him. "What do you want Me to do for you?" Jesus asked.

Bartimaeus didn't hesitate. "I want to see!" he said.

Jesus said, "Receive your sight. Your faith has healed you." Instantly, Bartimaeus could see.

Bartimaeus believed Jesus could heal him, and Jesus did. But sometimes we believe and we pray, and God doesn't heal our bodies. It's impossible for us to understand why. But when we pray, God always, always heals our hearts and souls. ▶ *MARK 10; LUKE 18*

🏃 **HERO TRAINING** While we can't understand why some are healed on this earth and some are not, God gives us some beautiful promises for the future. In heaven, we won't need bandages or tissues or even a flashlight. Read Revelation 21:4 and Revelation 22:5 to find out why.

🏃 **BE A HERO!**

When someone is sick or hurting, a simple card can brighten the day. Send a card to each person on your church's list of those who are sick. Include your favorite Bible verse and let them know you're praying for them. Heroes pray for healing.

WHAT DO YOU WANT ME TO DO?

LORD, PLEASE *LET ME SEE.*

JESUS RESTORED THE MAN'S SIGHT. THE MAN THEN FOLLOWED JESUS AS HE CONTINUED ON HIS JOURNEY.

Seeking and Saving

Zacchaeus—The Tree Climber

Are there some people in your life you just know will never follow Jesus? They're so mean or proud or unlikeable. You're sure there's no point in talking to them about Jesus. That's how people felt about Zacchaeus. But Jesus knew better.

You see, Zacchaeus was a tax collector. In fact, he was the chief tax collector in that area, and he was wealthy. People believed (and they may have been right!) that he got his wealth from cheating them on their taxes. They refused to have anything to do with Zacchaeus.

ZACCHAEUS, COME DOWN FROM THAT TREE.

JOB: CHIEF TAX COLLECTOR

WHERE: JERICHO

KEY TERM: SON OF MAN: ANOTHER PHRASE TO DESCRIBE THE MESSIAH, JESUS

"The Son of Man came to seek and to save the lost."

—LUKE 19:10 NIV

One day Zacchaeus heard that Jesus was coming to town. Zacchaeus wanted to see Him. But he was short, and no one would let him through. So Zacchaeus ran down the road and climbed up a sycamore tree to get a better look.

When Jesus reached that spot, He called out, "Zacchaeus, come down! I'm coming to your house today."

The crowd of people following Jesus became angry. Didn't Jesus know who this was? Why would He go to a sinner's house?

Zacchaeus heard the people and said, "I'll give half my goods to the poor. And if I've stolen from anyone, I'll pay it back four times."

Those people in the crowd didn't think Jesus should bother with someone like Zacchaeus. But Jesus came to save all sinners, even a cheat and thief like Zacchaeus. God's love and mercy are for everyone—and yours should be too. ▶ *LUKE 19*

🦸 BE A HERO!

Plant a tree in honor of Zacchaeus in your yard or in your community. Each time you see it, remember that Jesus came to offer His love and grace to all people. Heroes tell everyone about Jesus.

🏃 **HERO TRAINING** It's so easy to slap a label on people: nerd, popular, rich, poor, foreign. But in God's eyes, we are all the same: sinners who need His grace. Read 1 John 4:10–12. How does God feel about each and every person? How should we, then, treat each and every person?

The Better Thing

Mary—Who Listened to Jesus

I f you had to choose between going to school and robbing a bank, what would you do? Well . . . that's an easy choice, right? What if your choice was between studying the Bible with a friend or watching a movie with a friend? Watching a movie isn't a bad thing, but studying the Bible is even better. Some choices are obviously right or wrong, but others come down to what's best.

Two sisters, Mary and Martha, faced a choice between a good thing and a better thing. You see, Jesus was staying at their house. Martha chose to spend her day preparing the house and cooking a meal for Jesus and His disciples—a good thing. Mary chose to spend her day sitting at Jesus' feet and listening to Him teach—the better thing.

JESUS WAS FRIENDS WITH TWO SISTERS, MARTHA AND MARY. ONE DAY JESUS AND HIS DISCIPLES STOPPED TO VISIT.

"Martha, Martha, you are worried and upset about many things. Only one thing is important. Mary has chosen the better thing, and it will never be taken away from her."

—LUKE 10:41–42 NCV

WHO: MARY AND MARTHA (SISTERS OF LAZARUS AND FRIENDS OF JESUS)

WHERE: THE VILLAGE OF BETHANY, ABOUT TWO MILES FROM JERUSALEM

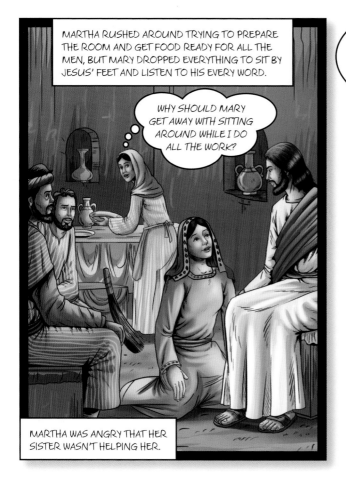

MARTHA RUSHED AROUND TRYING TO PREPARE THE ROOM AND GET FOOD READY FOR ALL THE MEN, BUT MARY DROPPED EVERYTHING TO SIT BY JESUS' FEET AND LISTEN TO HIS EVERY WORD.

WHY SHOULD MARY GET AWAY WITH SITTING AROUND WHILE I DO ALL THE WORK?

MARTHA WAS ANGRY THAT HER SISTER WASN'T HELPING HER.

MARTHA, MARTHA, YOU ARE WORRYING ABOUT LOTS OF THINGS, BUT ONLY ONE THING IS IMPORTANT. MARY HAS CHOSEN WHAT IS BETTER, AND IT WON'T BE TAKEN AWAY FROM HER.

Martha became upset. She was doing all the work while Mary was "just" sitting with Jesus. Jesus gently told Martha, "Mary has chosen what is better, and it won't be taken away from her." Martha's cooking and cleaning weren't wrong. They just weren't as important as spending time with Jesus.

When you face a choice between two good things, ask yourself this question: Which choice will help you spend more time with Jesus? ▶ *LUKE 10*

✗ HERO TRAINING Mary sat at Jesus' feet and listened to His words. You can too. Ask your parents to help you download an audio Bible app, and listen to one of your favorite passages.

🦸 BE A HERO!

Your parents do a lot for you. There are probably times when they feel like Martha, doing nonstop chores, and they wish they could be like Mary, sitting at Jesus' feet. Surprise them by doing a chore or two. Then invite them to read a Bible story with you. Heroes help others make time for Jesus.

Right on Time

Lazarus—The Raised

Have you ever done the exact right thing at the exact wrong time, like jumping up and cheering when the basketball swished through the net . . . only to realize it was the other team who scored? While we do that sort of thing sometimes, Jesus always does exactly the right thing at exactly the right time.

Mary and Martha believed this. That's why they were so confused when Jesus didn't come

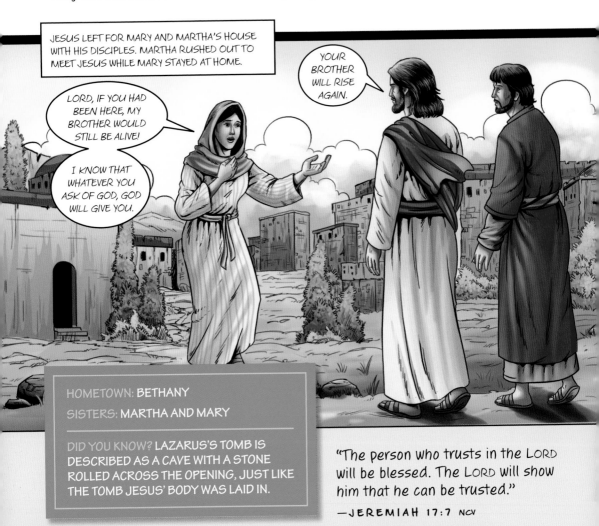

JESUS LEFT FOR MARY AND MARTHA'S HOUSE WITH HIS DISCIPLES. MARTHA RUSHED OUT TO MEET JESUS WHILE MARY STAYED AT HOME.

LORD, IF YOU HAD BEEN HERE, MY BROTHER WOULD STILL BE ALIVE!

I KNOW THAT WHATEVER YOU ASK OF GOD, GOD WILL GIVE YOU.

YOUR BROTHER WILL RISE AGAIN.

HOMETOWN: BETHANY

SISTERS: MARTHA AND MARY

DID YOU KNOW? LAZARUS'S TOMB IS DESCRIBED AS A CAVE WITH A STONE ROLLED ACROSS THE OPENING, JUST LIKE THE TOMB JESUS' BODY WAS LAID IN.

"The person who trusts in the LORD will be blessed. The LORD will show him that he can be trusted."
—JEREMIAH 17:7 NCV

to help right away. You see, they had sent a message that their brother, Lazarus—whom Jesus knew and loved—was very sick. But Jesus didn't come, and Lazarus died. In fact, Lazarus had been dead for four days when Jesus finally arrived. "If you had been here," Martha said, "my brother would still be alive!"

Mary also ran out to Jesus, weeping. Seeing her sorrow, Jesus wept too. And though it had already been four days, Jesus ordered them to open the tomb. "Come out, Lazarus!" He called. And Lazarus walked out of the tomb!

BE A HERO!

Even though God is never late, sometimes His heroes are. What should you do when you're running late? If possible, call ahead and let the person you're supposed to meet know you'll be late. Then apologize and do your best to not be late again!

Martha and Mary believed their brother died because Jesus was late. But Jesus was right on time for His purpose. Jesus wanted to show that God had the power to raise the dead. There will be times when God's answers seem late. But He is always right on time for His perfect purpose. ▶JOHN 11

HERO TRAINING The Bible says that there is a proper time for everything. Read Ecclesiastes 3:1–8 to discover all the different things that there are times for. When you're going through a tough time, what do these verses promise you?

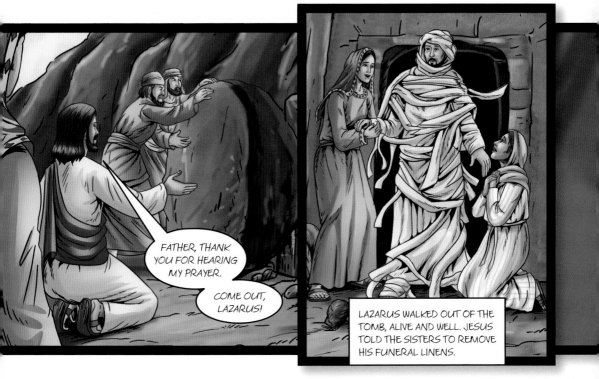

FATHER, THANK YOU FOR HEARING MY PRAYER.

COME OUT, LAZARUS!

LAZARUS WALKED OUT OF THE TOMB, ALIVE AND WELL. JESUS TOLD THE SISTERS TO REMOVE HIS FUNERAL LINENS.

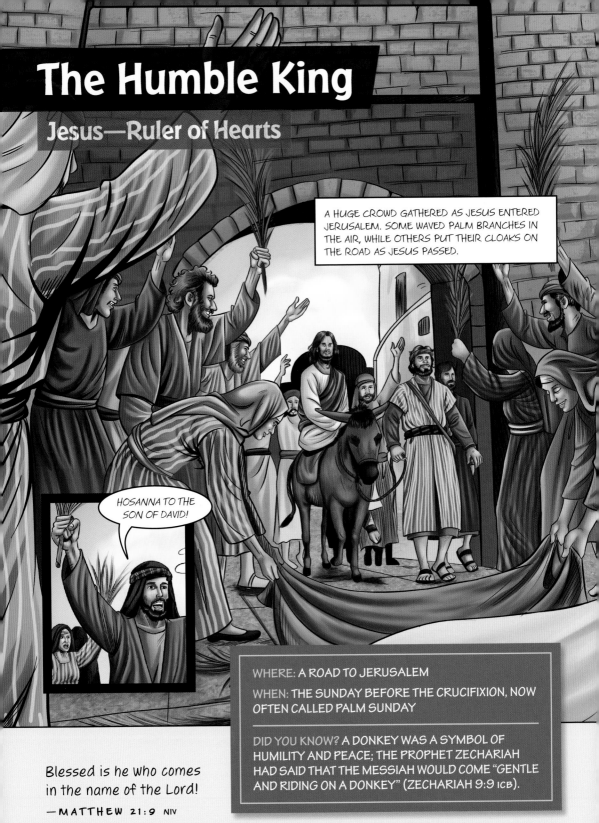

The Humble King

Jesus—Ruler of Hearts

A HUGE CROWD GATHERED AS JESUS ENTERED JERUSALEM. SOME WAVED PALM BRANCHES IN THE AIR, WHILE OTHERS PUT THEIR CLOAKS ON THE ROAD AS JESUS PASSED.

HOSANNA TO THE SON OF DAVID!

WHERE: A ROAD TO JERUSALEM

WHEN: THE SUNDAY BEFORE THE CRUCIFIXION, NOW OFTEN CALLED PALM SUNDAY

DID YOU KNOW? A DONKEY WAS A SYMBOL OF HUMILITY AND PEACE; THE PROPHET ZECHARIAH HAD SAID THAT THE MESSIAH WOULD COME "GENTLE AND RIDING ON A DONKEY" (ZECHARIAH 9:9 ICB).

Blessed is he who comes in the name of the Lord!

—MATTHEW 21:9 NIV

Have you ever expected one thing, but you got something so much better? Imagine ordering a cup of ice cream and getting a hot fudge sundae instead! Something even more surprising and wonderful happened to the Jewish people.

The Jews were expecting a Savior powerful enough to kick out the Romans and make Israel into a great nation again. But what they got was Jesus. He didn't come to kick out the Romans. He came for a greater purpose: to kick out

BLESSED IS HE WHO COMES IN THE NAME OF THE LORD!

sin and death and Satan. Jesus didn't come leading a powerful army. He came riding on the back of a donkey.

When Jesus entered Jerusalem that day, He expected to soon be arrested, beaten, and nailed to a cross. His followers were expecting very different things—amazing and miraculous things. So when they saw Him coming, huge crowds gathered. Some waved palm branches in the air to praise Him. Others threw down their cloaks on the road in front of Him. "Hosanna to the Son of David!" they shouted. "Blessed is He who comes in the name of the Lord. Hosanna in the highest heaven!"

The people were expecting an earthly king. They didn't understand that Jesus was the King of something far greater: a heavenly kingdom that would never end. You see, Jesus didn't come to rule the world; He came to rule your heart. ▶ *MATTHEW 21; MARK 11; LUKE 19*

🦸 BE A HERO!

Jesus often did the unexpected. Why not do something unexpected too? On a hot day, pass out free popsicles in your neighborhood (or hot chocolate on a winter's day). Heroes find opportunities every day to be kind and show God's love.

🦸 HERO TRAINING Jesus didn't come to be King of the world; He came to be King of your heart and life. How can you make Him your King? Obey Him! Read what Jesus says about the importance of obeying Him in Luke 6:46–49 and John 14:15.

Giving It All

A Widow—The Greatest Giver

When the collection plate goes around at church, what do you put in? Perhaps you drop in part of your allowance or some money your parents gave you. But imagine putting in every last cent your family has—so much that you don't even have money to buy lunch. That's exactly what one woman did.

ONE TIME JESUS WAS SITTING IN THE TEMPLE WITH SOME OF HIS DISCIPLES. HE WATCHED AS ALL THE RICH PEOPLE PUT GOLD AND SILVER INTO THE TEMPLE COLLECTION. BUT HE ALSO SAW A POOR WIDOW GIVING HER COPPER COINS.

WHO: A POOR WIDOW

WHERE: THE TEMPLE IN JERUSALEM

Each of you should give as you have decided in your heart to give. You should not be sad when you give, and you should not give because you feel forced to give. God loves the person who gives happily.

—2 CORINTHIANS 9:7 NCV

Jesus saw her as He was sitting in the temple. He had watched as rich people dropped their gold and silver into the temple collection. The collection boxes were shaped like trumpets, so the sound of the dropped coins echoed across the crowds.

Then Jesus saw a poor widow drop in two small copper coins. They barely made a sound. Yet Jesus praised the woman. "This poor widow has given more than all the others."

How could that be? The woman had only given two small coins. But it was all she had to give. In the eyes of the world and those rich people, the widow's gift didn't matter. But Jesus said hers was the greatest gift of all.

Jesus not only sees what you give; He also sees how you give. He knows when you give just because you have to. And He knows when you give happily, because you want to give back to the One who has given you so much. That's the kind of giving He blesses.
▶ *MARK 12; LUKE 21*

⟟ BE A HERO!

Ask your parents to help you come up with a plan to give back to God. Make sure your plan isn't just for money. Find ways to give your time and talents too. And check your attitude—God loves when you give joyfully!

🏃 **HERO TRAINING** Some people, like the Pharisees, wanted to be sure everyone could see what they gave. But read Matthew 6:1–4 to see what Jesus had to say about that. How does Jesus want you to give?

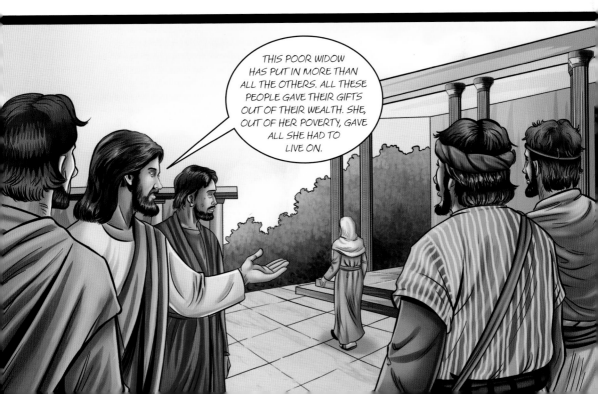

THIS POOR WIDOW HAS PUT IN MORE THAN ALL THE OTHERS. ALL THESE PEOPLE GAVE THEIR GIFTS OUT OF THEIR WEALTH. SHE, OUT OF HER POVERTY, GAVE ALL SHE HAD TO LIVE ON.

Anointing the Savior

Mary—Who Did What She Could

WHY IS THAT WOMAN WASTING SUCH EXPENSIVE OIL? IT COULD HAVE BEEN SOLD TO FEED THE POOR!

ONE DAY, WHEN JESUS WAS VISITING THE HOUSE OF SIMON THE LEPER IN BETHANY, A WOMAN CAME WITH A JAR OF PERFUMED OIL AND GENTLY POURED IT ON HIS HEAD.

SIBLINGS: MARTHA AND LAZARUS

WHERE: BETHANY, AT THE HOME OF SIMON THE LEPER, PROBABLY SOMEONE JESUS HAD HEALED EARLIER

WHEN: THE WEEK BEFORE THE CROSS

Give to the LORD the glory he deserves!
—1 CHRONICLES 16:29 NLT

Like the wind, love is something you can't actually see. But you can see what love does and the way it touches and changes people.

Mary loved Jesus. She knew He was from God. And while she didn't know about the cross and all that was coming, she may have known Jesus was in danger. The chief priests and the Pharisees all wanted Him dead.

So when Jesus came to the home of Simon the Leper, Mary couldn't miss the chance to show Jesus how much she loved Him. Taking a jar of perfume, she broke it open and gently poured it on Jesus' head. Some scolded her harshly because the perfume was expensive and could have been sold to help the poor.

But Jesus knew Mary's heart. He said, "Leave her alone. She has done a beautiful thing. The poor will always be with you, but you will not always have Me. She did what she could. She prepared My body for burial. Wherever the gospel is preached, what she has done will be told."

Mary couldn't stop the people who hated Jesus. But she could show Him her love. In the same way, you can't stop those who hate Jesus today, but you can show Him your love. Don't stop to count the cost of what others will think or say—declare your love for Jesus. Like Mary, do what you can do. ▶MARK 14

🏃 **HERO TRAINING** Your prayers and praises are like a sweet perfume to the Lord (Psalm 141:2). Anoint Him with your love by declaring His praises. Use the words of Psalm 145 to tell the Lord how wonderful He is. Or write your own words of love to Him.

🦸 BE A HERO!

How can you show love to Jesus? Matthew 25:35-40 tells you: be His hands and feet. Feed the hungry, clothe the poor, take care of the sick and those in prison. Heroes do what they can!

LEAVE HER ALONE. SHE HAS DONE A GOOD THING. THE POOR YOU WILL ALWAYS HAVE, BUT YOU WILL NOT ALWAYS HAVE ME. SHE IS ANOINTING MY BODY FOR BURIAL.

"Do as I Have Done"

Jesus—The Servant Savior

WHILE THEY WERE ALL SITTING DOWN, JESUS WRAPPED A TOWEL AROUND HIS WAIST, POURED WATER IN A BOWL, AND ONE BY ONE, HE BEGAN TO WASH THE FEET OF THE DISCIPLES AND DRY THEM WITH THE TOWEL.

WHO: JESUS AND HIS DISCIPLES

WHERE: JERUSALEM

WHEN: THE PASSOVER MEAL ON THE THURSDAY BEFORE THE CROSS; OFTEN CALLED "THE LAST SUPPER"

"For even the Son of Man came not to be served but to serve others and to give his life as a ransom for many."

—MARK 10:45 NLT

Imagine you and your friends are at a party. You go to throw away your cup, but the trash can is overflowing. It's smelly and nasty. Surely someone else is supposed to take care of it. After all, you're here to have fun, not to clean up after everyone else, right?

That's probably about what the disciples were thinking when they sat down to the Passover meal. Their feet were smelly and dirty from walking on dusty roads in sandals. It was a servant's job to wash their feet—they wouldn't think of doing it themselves.

The meal had already started when Jesus got up and wrapped a towel around His waist. He knew the cross was coming. He didn't have much time left to teach His disciples. But He used His last night to give them a very important lesson—He knelt down and washed His disciples' feet. Peter was shocked. This was too dirty of a job for his Savior!

"I'm giving you an example," Jesus explained. "If I, your Teacher, have washed your feet, then you also should wash one another's feet. Do as I have done to you."

Jesus is the Son of God. But He didn't come to be served. He came to serve His people. So don't expect others to serve you. Be like Jesus. Be willing to serve. ▶JOHN 13

🏃 HERO TRAINING Philippians 2:5–8 is one of the most beautiful descriptions of what Jesus did for us. What did Jesus give up to come to us?

SIMON PETER WAS HORRIFIED WHEN JESUS KNELT BEFORE HIM TO WASH HIS FEET.

JESUS EXPLAINED THAT HE WAS SETTING AN EXAMPLE FOR THEM.

LORD, I CAN'T LET YOU WASH MY FEET!

IF I, YOUR TEACHER, HAVE WASHED YOUR FEET, THEN YOU ALSO OUGHT TO WASH ONE ANOTHER'S FEET. DO AS I HAVE DONE TO YOU!

The First Lord's Supper

Jesus—The Bread

JESUS AND THE DISCIPLES BEGAN TO EAT THE PASSOVER MEAL.

TAKE AND EAT; THIS IS MY BODY.

WHEN: THE PASSOVER MEAL, OR "LAST SUPPER"; THE THURSDAY BEFORE THE CRUCIFIXION

DID YOU KNOW? THE TRADITIONAL PASSOVER MEAL INCLUDES BREAD, WINE, BITTER HERBS, AND A LAMB.

Every time you eat this bread and drink this cup, you show others about the Lord's death until he comes.

—1 CORINTHIANS 11:26 ICB

How do you celebrate holidays? Do you have a big dinner and invite your family and friends? People in Bible times often remembered holidays with a feast. Before the cross, Jesus celebrated the Passover with His disciples. But He also used the symbols of the holiday meal—the bread and the wine—to prepare His followers to remember Him and all that He was about to do for them.

It was the last meal Jesus would share with His disciples before the cross. He looked around the table at these men He'd spent the last three years teaching, then He lifted up the bread. He thanked God for it, broke it, and gave pieces to His disciples. "This is My body," He said. "Take and eat. Do this to remember Me." Then Jesus took a cup and gave thanks for it. He passed it around to His disciples also. "Drink," He said. "This is My blood, which is poured out for the forgiveness of your sins. This begins the new agreement between God and His people."

The disciples did as Jesus told them, though they didn't yet understand all that it meant. You see, sin must be punished. So Jesus—the One who never sinned—took all the world's sins with Him to the cross. There, His body was punished for our sins, and His blood was spilled to wash them away.

At that first Lord's Supper, Jesus said, "Do this to remember Me." When you become a follower of Christ, you, too, will take the Lord's Supper (sometimes called communion) and remember all that Jesus has done for you.
▶ MATTHEW 26; MARK 14; LUKE 22

🦸 HERO TRAINING After that Last Supper, Jesus and His disciples sang hymns together. Tradition says they sang hymns from Psalms 115–118. Read these psalms for yourself, and think about the night Jesus and His disciples sang them together.

🦸 BE A HERO!

Jesus gave thanks before He broke the bread. Each time you sit down to eat, remember to thank God for the food and all the other blessings He gives you. Heroes remember. And they give thanks.

TAKE THIS CUP, AND DRINK FROM IT, FOR THIS IS MY BLOOD.

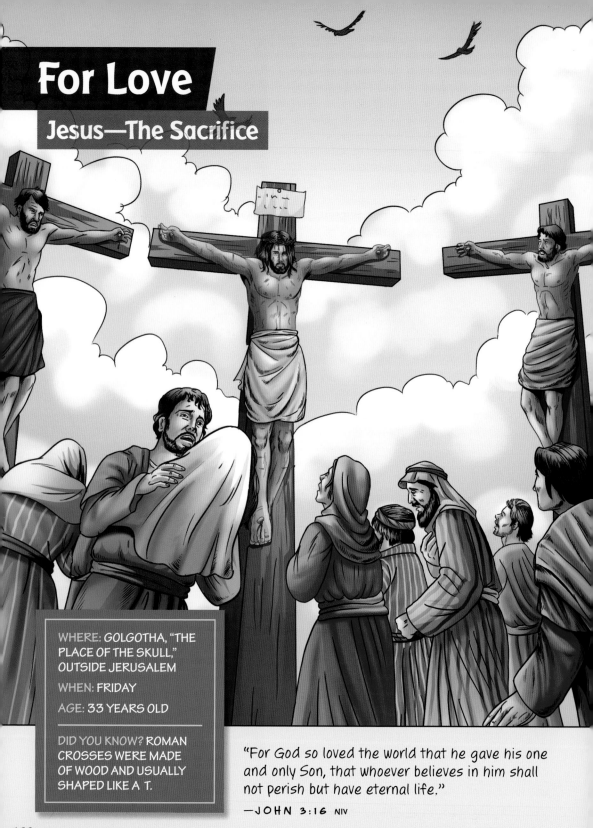

For Love

Jesus—The Sacrifice

WHERE: GOLGOTHA, "THE PLACE OF THE SKULL," OUTSIDE JERUSALEM

WHEN: FRIDAY

AGE: 33 YEARS OLD

DID YOU KNOW? ROMAN CROSSES WERE MADE OF WOOD AND USUALLY SHAPED LIKE A T.

"For God so loved the world that he gave his one and only Son, that whoever believes in him shall not perish but have eternal life."

—JOHN 3:16 NIV

How often do you ask *why*? It's a popular question. We ask why about big things, like why bad things happen to good people. And we ask why about small things, like why we have to go to bed so early. But the most important of all these why questions is "Why did Jesus die?"

The hour had finally come. After that last meal together, there had been prayers, a betrayal and arrest, phony trials, and beatings. Then Roman soldiers nailed Jesus to a cross and stood it up on a hill between two crucified criminals. They made fun of Him and spat on Him.

Darkness covered the land as God the Father turned away from His only Son, unable to look at the sin Jesus had taken upon Himself. "My God, My God, why have you left Me alone?" Jesus cried out. Then He gave up His Spirit and took His last breath.

The One who had never, ever sinned took the punishment for all our sins. In those same moments, the temple curtain—the curtain that separated people from the Holy of Holies—was torn in two, from top to bottom. The ripped cloth was a beautiful symbol for what Jesus came to do: tear down the wall of sin that separates people from God.

Because Jesus died on the cross, our sins can be forgiven, we can be made holy, and we can step right into the presence of God with our prayers. Why? Why did Jesus do this? The answer only needs one word: *love.* ▶ *MATTHEW 27; MARK 15; LUKE 23; JOHN 18–19*

🦸 BE A HERO!

For love, Jesus died on a cross. What will you do for love? Will you declare your love for Jesus and risk being made fun of? Will you tell someone about Jesus and risk being rejected? Will you risk trusting Him with your whole heart? Because heroes love Jesus—no matter the risk.

🦸 HERO TRAINING Look up John 3:16. Who spoke those words? Read verses 1–21 of that same chapter. Who was He talking to? Now look up John 19:38–40. Do you think Nicodemus became a follower of Jesus?

He is not here; he has risen, just as he said.

—MATTHEW 28:6 NIV

MARY RUSHED TO TELL PETER AND JOHN ABOUT THE EMPTY TOMB. PETER AND JOHN RUSHED TO THE TOMB. INSIDE THEY FOUND ONLY THE DISCARDED CLOTH THAT HAD BEEN USED TO WRAP JESUS' BODY. THE TOMB WAS EMPTY!

THE DISCIPLES WERE FILLED WITH AWE.

magine how you would feel if a treasure you thought you had lost forever was suddenly found. That's just a taste of what Mary Magdalene and the others felt as they stood in front of Jesus' tomb.

It was the Sunday morning after the crucifixion. Filled with sorrow, Mary Magdalene and the other women were on their way to the tomb. They wondered who would roll the stone away for them, but when they arrived, the stone had already been moved. The tomb was empty! *Did someone steal Jesus' body?* the women wondered.

Then suddenly, two angels appeared. "Jesus isn't here," they said. "He is risen, just as He promised! Go and tell the others." Mary raced to tell Peter and John. They, in turn, ran to see the empty tomb with their own eyes.

Meanwhile, Mary stood outside the tomb alone, weeping. She didn't understand all that had happened. All she knew was that her Savior was gone. Then suddenly—He wasn't! Jesus was right there, calling her name. "Mary," He said. She couldn't run fast enough to tell the others she had just seen Jesus.

Jesus died to take away our sins. He rose again to show that death had no hold on Him—or on those who follow Him. Because of Jesus, you can one day rise up to heaven and live for eternity with Him. ▶*MATTHEW 27–28; MARK 15–16; LUKE 23–24; JOHN 19–20*

🏃 HERO TRAINING The same powerful God who raised Jesus from the dead is working in your life. Look up 2 Corinthians 4:14 to see what He promises to those who follow Jesus.

👤 BE A HERO!

When she heard Jesus call her by name, Mary knew she was important to Him. Using someone's name can make someone feel seen, known, and loved. So learn the name of everyone in your church. Then use their names when you speak to them. Heroes make everyone feel loved and important.

On the Road

Jesus—Keeper of Promises

Have you ever heard the saying "put two and two together"? It means using what you know to figure out what's happened. For example, if your sister can't resist cupcakes and there's a cupcake missing, you might "put two and two together" to figure out that your sister ate the missing cupcake!

Jesus' followers were having trouble putting two and two together. Even though Jesus had risen from the grave, some still didn't understand that He was the promised Messiah.

The day Jesus rose, two of those followers were walking along the road to Emmaus. As they talked about all that had happened, Jesus came up to them, but they didn't recognize Him. Jesus asked what they were talking about. "Haven't you heard about all

> HOW SLOW YOU ARE TO BELIEVE WHAT THE PROPHETS HAVE TOLD YOU! DIDN'T THE MESSIAH HAVE TO SUFFER THESE THINGS AND THEN BEGIN HIS TIME OF GLORY?

> AND BEGINNING WITH MOSES AND ALL THE PROPHETS, HE EXPLAINED TO THEM WHAT WAS SAID IN ALL THE SCRIPTURES CONCERNING HIMSELF. BUT THE MEN DID NOT RECOGNIZE HIM.

WHO: CLEOPAS AND ANOTHER FOLLOWER OF JESUS

WHERE: ON THE ROAD TO EMMAUS, A SMALL VILLAGE OUTSIDE JERUSALEM

You are blessed because you believed that what the Lord said to you would really happen.
—LUKE 1:45 NCV

that happened to Jesus?" they exclaimed. "He was a mighty prophet!"

But Jesus was much more than a prophet. He was the Messiah. So Jesus explained to them the Old Testament scriptures that told about Him. Later, when they sat down to dinner, Jesus took the bread, gave thanks, and broke it. In that moment, they saw that it was Jesus! Instantly, Jesus disappeared, and they ran back to Jerusalem to tell the others what had happened.

God gave hundreds of prophecies and promises in the Old Testament about the coming Messiah. And Jesus kept every single one of them. What does that say about the promises God gives you in the Bible? He'll keep every single one of them too!

▶ *Luke 24*

✝ BE A HERO!

Jesus shared His message while traveling along the road. You can do the same. As you travel along—whether it's on the bus to school, in the car with friends, or on a bike ride around your neighborhood—talk about Jesus. Share your favorite Bible verse or worship song. Tell your friends what Jesus means to you and how much He loves them.

HERO TRAINING The Old Testament has over three hundred prophecies about the coming of the Messiah. Read Isaiah 53, one of the most well known. In what ways do you see this prophecy coming true in Jesus?

AS THE STRANGER BROKE BREAD, CLEOPAS AND HIS FRIEND REALIZED WHO THE STRANGER WAS.

MY LORD, IT IS YOU!

JESUS VANISHED AS SOON AS CLEOPAS AND HIS FRIEND RECOGNIZED HIM.

CLEOPAS AND HIS FRIEND RACED TO JERUSALEM TO TELL THE OTHERS WHAT THEY HAD SEEN.

WHEN HE SPOKE TO US, IT WAS AS IF OUR HEARTS WERE ON FIRE!

THE LORD IS RISEN INDEED!

Seeing the Savior

Jesus—The Seen

PEACE BE WITH YOU.

IT'S A GHOST!

THE DISCIPLES WERE FRIGHTENED. SOME THOUGHT THEY WERE SEEING A GHOST.

WHO: JESUS AND HIS DISCIPLES

WHERE: HIDING BEHIND LOCKED DOORS

WHEN: SUNDAY EVENING, AFTER THE RESURRECTION

Jesus told him, "You believe because you see me. Those who believe without seeing me will be truly blessed."

—JOHN 20:29 NCV

Faith is believing something will happen. For example, you might believe you'll see the beach because your parents say that's where you're going for vacation. When you get to the beach, your faith is rewarded by seeing the ocean. Faith in Jesus works the same way. We believe His promises of heaven, knowing that one day we will see them come true with our own eyes.

But Jesus' disciples were struggling with their faith. They had believed Jesus was the Messiah, until they had seen Him killed. Now, though His tomb was empty, they still weren't sure what to believe. On top of that, they were afraid the Jewish leaders would come after them too. So they were hiding in a locked house.

Then suddenly, Jesus Himself stood among them and said, "Peace be with you."

The disciples were startled and scared. *Is this a ghost?*

"Why are you troubled? Why do you doubt?" Jesus asked. "Look at My hands and My feet." He showed them His wounds from the nails. "Touch Me," He said. "A ghost does not have flesh and bones!" Still, it was too wonderful for the disciples to believe. So Jesus asked, "Do you have anything to eat?" They gave Him a piece of fish, which He ate. Then they believed.

The disciples believed because they saw the risen Jesus with their own eyes. As His followers, we have faith that Jesus is alive and will keep His promises. And one day we'll see Him with our own eyes too.
▶ *Luke 24; John 20*

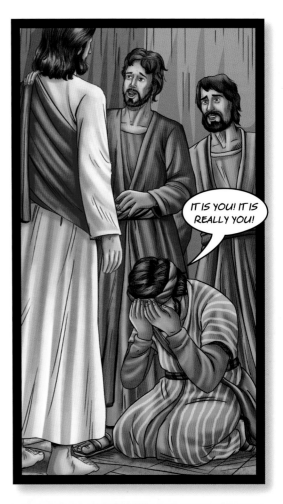

IT IS YOU! IT IS REALLY YOU!

🏃 HERO TRAINING One day we will see Jesus face-to-face with our own eyes (Revelation 22:1–4). What do you imagine that will be like? What do you think you will do first? Will you bow before Him or run to hug Him or something else?

⚡ BE A HERO!

Right now, no one on earth can see Jesus in person. But your face can show the love of Jesus to the world. Make it part of your mission to smile when you meet other kids at school. And if they ask why, take that opportunity to tell them about Jesus, the One who makes you smile.

"Do You Love Me?"

Peter—The Forgiven

Have you ever made a mistake so big you had trouble forgiving yourself? But then the person you let down or hurt forgave you. How wonderful did that feel? Peter knew both the shame of a mistake and the wonder of being forgiven.

WHEN THE MEN FINISHED THEIR MEAL, JESUS SPOKE TO PETER.

SIMON PETER, DO YOU LOVE ME?

YES, LORD. YOU KNOW THAT I LOVE YOU.

Peter's huge mistake was denying Jesus. After Jesus was arrested, Peter followed Him, trying to blend in with the crowd of people. But some people thought

FEED MY LAMBS.

JOB: FISHERMAN

WHERE: BY THE SEA OF GALILEE

WHEN: SHORTLY AFTER THE RESURRECTION

DID YOU KNOW? THE DISCIPLES CAUGHT 153 FISH THAT DAY.

Be kind and loving to each other. Forgive each other just as God forgave you in Christ.
—EPHESIANS 4:32 ICB

they recognized him as one of Jesus' follow-ers. Afraid of what they would do to him, Peter denied even knowing Jesus—not just once, not twice, but three times. Later, when he realized what he had done, Peter wept.

After His resurrection, Jesus came out to the Sea of Galilee. Peter and the others had been fishing all night but hadn't caught a thing. Jesus called out, "Throw your nets out on the right side of the boat." The disciples did and caught so many fish they couldn't pull the nets into the boat. That's when Peter knew it was his Lord. He jumped out of the boat and swam to shore.

Jesus met Peter with breakfast and three questions: Three times Jesus asked Peter if he loved Him. Three times Peter said yes. And three times Jesus told Peter to feed His sheep.

What did all that mean? It meant Peter was completely and perfectly forgiven and that he was tasked with teaching the good news to God's followers (the sheep, as Jesus is the Shepherd). When you mess up—and everyone does—run to Jesus, just as Peter did. And you will be completely forgiven too. ▶JOHN 18, 21

🏃 HERO TRAINING Three times Peter denied knowing Jesus after His arrest. Three times Jesus gave Peter the chance to say he loved Him. And three times Jesus gave Peter a role in His kingdom. Even when you mess up, Jesus has a purpose and a place for you. Check out His amazing promise in 2 Timothy 2:21.

Home to Heaven

Jesus—The Ascended

JESUS WAS LIFTED UP TO HEAVEN, AND A CLOUD HID HIM FROM SIGHT.

WHERE: NEAR BETHANY

WHEN: 40 DAYS AFTER THE RESURRECTION

KEY TERM: ASCEND: TO RISE UP

DID YOU KNOW? ALL 12 DISCIPLES WERE FROM GALILEE, EXCEPT JUDAS.

"From now on, the Son of Man will be seated at the right hand of the mighty God."

—LUKE 22:69 NIV

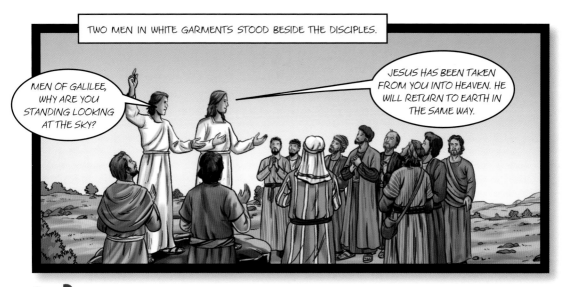

TWO MEN IN WHITE GARMENTS STOOD BESIDE THE DISCIPLES.

MEN OF GALILEE, WHY ARE YOU STANDING LOOKING AT THE SKY?

JESUS HAS BEEN TAKEN FROM YOU INTO HEAVEN. HE WILL RETURN TO EARTH IN THE SAME WAY.

Have you ever said good-bye to a friend who moved away? Maybe you thought, *I'll never see him again*. It's a terrible feeling, isn't it? And it's very different from saying good-bye to a friend going on vacation. Knowing you'll see your friend again makes saying good-bye much easier.

The disciples had said good-bye to Jesus at the cross. They had thought it would be forever. But after Jesus rose from the grave, He met with His followers for forty days, proving that He really was alive. Now it was time to return to the Father. This time, Jesus' disciples understood that He was the Messiah and that He would be coming back.

As Jesus said good-bye, He promised that the Holy Spirit would come. And He told the disciples to take His message to the ends of the earth. Still speaking, Jesus rose up into the clouds and out of sight. The disciples were gazing up after Him when suddenly two men dressed in white stood before them. "Why are you standing here, looking up into the sky?" they said. "Jesus has been taken into heaven. He will come back in the way you have seen Him go."

For those who follow Jesus, good-byes aren't forever. *Good-bye* really means "until we meet again in heaven." ▶*LUKE 24; ACTS 1*

🏃 **HERO TRAINING** When Jesus rose into heaven, He returned home to His Father. Take a look at Revelation 21. What will heaven be like? According to John 14:6, what is the only way to get there?

🦸 BE A HERO!

Heaven is your true home, but you can make your home on earth a more heavenly place. Use Bible verses to decorate your room and fill the house with songs of praise. But most of all, fill your home with the love and kindness of Christ. Every hero needs a "heavenly" home.

A Gift from God

The Holy Spirit—The Helper

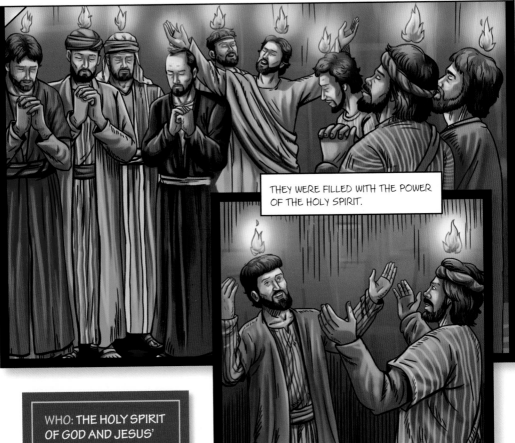

THE DISCIPLES HEARD A GREAT NOISE AS IF A HOWLING WIND WAS BLOWING THROUGH THE HOUSE. THEN BEFORE THEM THEY SAW WHAT SEEMED TO BE TONGUES OF FIRE THAT CAME TO REST ON EACH OF THEM.

THEY WERE FILLED WITH THE POWER OF THE HOLY SPIRIT.

WHO: THE HOLY SPIRIT OF GOD AND JESUS' FOLLOWERS

WHERE: JERUSALEM

WHEN: THE DAY OF PENTECOST, A JEWISH HARVEST FESTIVAL 50 DAYS AFTER THE PASSOVER SABBATH

"I will ask the Father, and he will give you another Helper to be with you forever—the Spirit of truth. The world cannot accept him, because it does not see him or know him. But you know him, because he lives with you and he will be in you."

—JOHN 14:16-17 NCV

When you've got a big job to do, it's wonderful to have someone to help you. Someone who knows the right way to do things. Someone who will encourage you to do your best. Someone who will always be there for you.

That's exactly what Jesus promised His disciples—a Helper. Jesus had big plans for His disciples, and they were going to need all the help they could get!

Just a few days after Jesus returned to heaven, the disciples were gathered together. They were celebrating the feast of Pentecost. Suddenly a great noise like a howling wind roared through the house. Tongues of fire hovered over each disciple's head. And they were filled with the power of the promised Helper: the Holy Spirit.

The Spirit's power allowed the disciples to speak in other languages. They told the gathering crowd about Jesus. And no matter what language people spoke, they understood. The Spirit's power also helped Peter powerfully share the good news of Jesus. About three thousand people became followers of Jesus that day. The power of the Holy Spirit transformed Peter from a fisherman to a fisher of men.

That same power is available to you. When you choose to follow and obey Jesus, the Helper—the Holy Spirit—comes to live and work inside you too. ▶Acts 2

BE A HERO!

The Holy Spirit came to help God's people. He encourages. He reminds us of Bible verses to guide us. He prays for us. Let the Holy Spirit use you to do those same things for others. Heroes let the Spirit work through them.

HERO TRAINING To find out more about the Holy Spirit, look up John 14:26 and Romans 8:26. What are some of the things the Holy Spirit does for us?

PETER STEPPED FORWARD AND ADDRESSED THE CROWD.

THE HOLY SPIRIT IS UPON US JUST AS THE PROPHET JOEL FORETOLD.

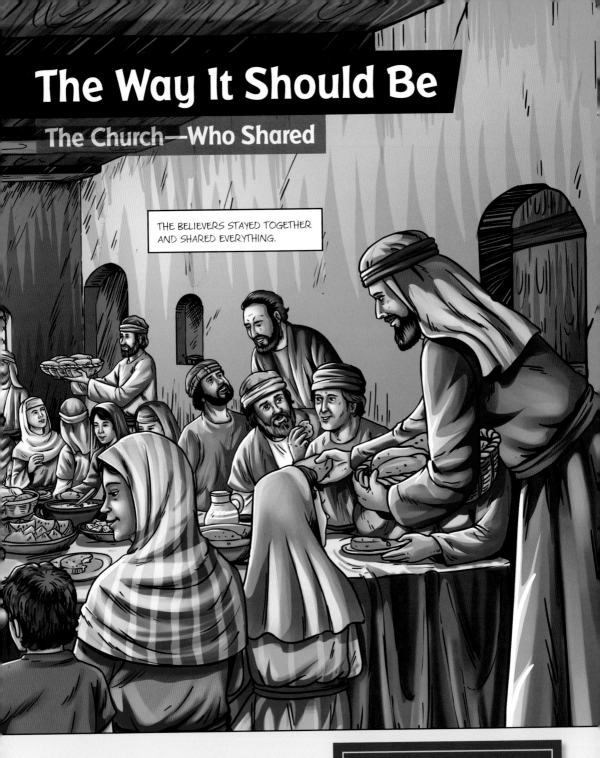

The Way It Should Be

The Church—Who Shared

THE BELIEVERS STAYED TOGETHER AND SHARED EVERYTHING.

All the believers were together and shared everything.

—ACTS 2:44 NCV

WHO: THE FOLLOWERS OF JESUS
WHERE: JERUSALEM

How do you feel about sharing? Not just your things or your food, but also your time, your talents, your home. That's what the first church of the New Testament did. They shared everything.

After Peter spoke at Pentecost, the new believers needed somewhere they could share their faith. So they gathered together to form a church. They studied all that the disciples taught them. They took the Lord's Supper and remembered all that Jesus had done for them. Those who were rich sold what they didn't need and gave it to those who were poor. They met in the temple courts and in each other's homes. They ate together, prayed together, and praised together. And because of their great love for God and each other, more and more people were saved each day.

That New Testament church didn't just share their food, their money, and their possessions. They shared friendship and fellowship. They shared laughter and prayers. They shared life. Learn to love and share with those in your church. A life lived among God's people is a beautiful thing, no matter what century you're living in! ▶Acts 2

BE A HERO!

The members of the early church sold what they could and gave it to those who had nothing. Ask a parent's permission to gather up what you don't need or use and hold a garage sale. Give the money you earn to your church to help the poor.

🏃 HERO TRAINING Read Hebrews 13:16. What two things does this verse say to do? Now read the end of the verse again. Doing these things pleases God!

Leaping for Joy!

Peter—The Spirit-Filled

What makes you want to leap for joy? Maybe it's enjoying a birthday cake, acing a test, or making the perfect shot. Or perhaps it's something more personal like a note from a friend, an "I love you," or seeing someone special.

For a beggar sitting outside the temple, it was a chance at a whole new life that made him leap for joy. You see, every day he was carried to the temple gate to beg for coins. He had to be carried because he couldn't walk.

BY THE POWER OF JESUS CHRIST—STAND UP AND WALK!

PETER TOOK THE MAN'S HAND AND LIFTED HIM UP.

LOOK AT ME! LOOK AT ME! I CAN DANCE!

WHO: PETER AND JOHN

WHERE: THE TEMPLE IN JERUSALEM, AT THE BEAUTIFUL GATE, THE MOST POPULAR ENTRANCE INTO THE TEMPLE

You are God's children. That is why God sent the Spirit of his Son into your hearts. The Spirit cries out, "Father, dear Father."

—GALATIANS 4:6 ICB

One day this beggar asked Peter and John for money. Peter didn't hesitate. He looked straight at him and said, "Look at us!" The man looked up, expecting coins. Instead, Peter said, "I don't have gold or silver, but I'll give you what I do have. In the name of Jesus Christ of Nazareth, get up and walk!" Then, taking his hand, Peter pulled the man to his feet.

The man walked around and jumped and praised God! Everyone who saw him was amazed. Peter took the chance to teach the gathered crowd about Jesus.

BE A HERO!

Jesus is the Great Physician, but you can help by being prepared for little emergencies. Assemble a family first-aid kit with bandages, disinfectant, tape, and more (visit RedCross.org for ideas). Put everything inside a box. Then decorate the outside with the words of Psalm 147:3.

The beggar's healing was nothing short of amazing! But even though Peter said the words, did he heal the man? No! Peter simply shared the most valuable thing he had—the power of Jesus given to him through the Holy Spirit. And here's something just as amazing: when you follow Jesus, that same Spirit lives and works inside you! ▶Acts 3

HERO TRAINING

Notice what Peter said to the beggar: "In the name of Jesus Christ of Nazareth." Peter didn't take credit for the man's healing. He knew—and he wanted the world to know—that the power of healing came from the risen Christ working through the Spirit of God. And that Spirit was in Peter. Read Psalm 150 and remember: heroes always give credit to God.

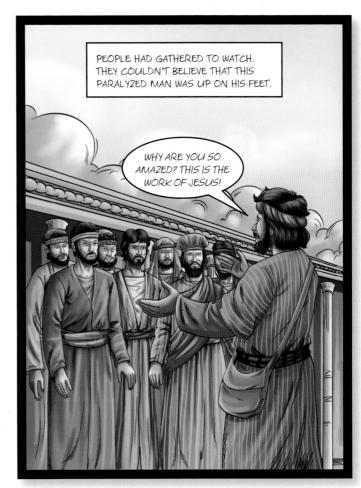

PEOPLE HAD GATHERED TO WATCH. THEY COULDN'T BELIEVE THAT THIS PARALYZED MAN WAS UP ON HIS FEET.

WHY ARE YOU SO AMAZED? THIS IS THE WORK OF JESUS!

If It Were Easy

Stephen—The Martyr

"I have told you these things, so that in me you may have peace. In this world you will have trouble. But take heart! I have overcome the world."

—JOHN 16:33 NIV

You've probably heard the saying, "If it were easy, everyone would do it." Whether it's playing the piano, running in the Olympics, or acing the science test, there's a lot of truth in that saying. It's also true when it comes to living out your faith in Jesus.

Stephen lived his life for Jesus, even when his life was in danger. You see, the disciples had chosen Stephen to help them lead the church. And through the power of the Spirit, Stephen had performed miracles.

LORD, DO NOT HOLD THIS AGAINST THEM!

EVEN THEN, STEPHEN'S LAST THOUGHTS WERE NOT OF HIMSELF.

But not everyone was happy about that. Stephen was hauled before the Jewish court. There, people told lies about him—just as they had about Jesus. Instead of trying to defend himself, Stephen preached about his Savior.

The members of the court were furious. But Stephen was full of the Holy Spirit. He looked up to heaven and said, "I see heaven open and the Son of Man standing at the right hand of God." With that, Stephen was dragged out of the city and stoned. Even as he died, Stephen tried to be like Jesus. He said, "Lord, do not hold this sin against them."

Jesus never promised that living for Him would be easy. In fact, He said just the opposite. Jesus knew we would have troubles in this world. But look at what else He said: "I have overcome the world." And when you follow Him, He'll help you overcome it too.

▶ ACTS 6–7

HERO TRAINING Take a close look at Acts 7:57–58. When Stephen was stoned, people laid their coats at whose feet? Remember that name. You'll see it again when Jesus stops him on the road to Damascus!

BE A HERO!

It would be easier to ignore someone being picked on rather than to defend him. It would be easier to keep quiet when people make fun of others. It would be easier to fit in by doing things you know are wrong. But heroes don't take the easy way out. Heroes stand up for God.

Sharing the Good News

Philip—Teacher on the Go

Do you like sharing? If you're like most people, it depends on what you're asked to share! Spinach? Help yourself! But a hot fudge sundae? Hmm, maybe not. We all have things we don't mind sharing and other things we'd rather keep for ourselves. But our greatest treasure—Jesus—is something we should always be willing to share.

AS HE WALKED, PHILIP MET AN ETHIOPIAN OFFICIAL ON HIS WAY HOME FROM JERUSALEM, WHERE HE HAD GONE TO PRAY. HE WAS READING FROM THE BOOK OF ISAIAH.

SIR, YOU LOOK PUZZLED. CAN I HELP?

CAN YOU EXPLAIN THIS TO ME?

JOB: CHURCH LEADER; CHOSEN BY THE 12 DISCIPLES TO TAKE CARE OF THE NEEDY IN THE CHURCH

WHERE: A DESERT ROAD ON THE WAY FROM JERUSALEM TO GAZA

"Go and make followers of all people in the world. Baptize them in the name of the Father and the Son and the Holy Spirit. Teach them to obey everything that I have told you."

—MATTHEW 28:19-20 ICB

Philip was ready to share Jesus. But he didn't know where he was going or who he would be sharing with. You see, an angel told Philip to go to the desert road. So, knowing nothing more, Philip went.

On the road, Philip saw an Ethiopian man in a chariot. As he got closer, Philip realized the man was reading from the book of Isaiah. "Do you understand what you are reading?" Philip asked. The man didn't, and he invited Philip to climb up in the chariot and explain. Philip started with that very passage—a prophecy about the Messiah—and told the man the good news about Jesus.

As they traveled along, they came to some water. The man said, "Look! Here is water. What is stopping me from being baptized?" The chariot was stopped, and Philip baptized the Ethiopian. Then suddenly the Spirit whisked Philip away, and the Ethiopian went on his way, rejoicing.

That Ethiopian man became a follower of Jesus that day. And he probably went home to tell many more people about the Savior. All because Philip was willing to share his greatest treasure. Just imagine what God can do with you if you're willing to share Jesus too! ▶ACTS 8

BE A HERO!

Have you ever thought about how not telling people about Jesus is a selfish thing? Look at 2 Corinthians 4:7. God has given you a great treasure. It would be selfish not to share it! Find at least one person to share Jesus with this week.

🏃 HERO TRAINING When you want to share Jesus with someone, you may not always have your Bible with you. Memorize verses like John 3:16, 1 Corinthians 13:4-7, and Acts 2:38, along with your favorite verses. When you keep the Bible in your heart, you're always ready to share Jesus.

A Gift to Give

Tabitha—The Giver

Did you know that when you become a Christian, you get a gift? You do—a spiritual gift! This gift is the power to honor God in a special way, and not everyone is given the same one. Some people have the gift of teaching about God. Others have the gift of encouragement or of making peace. Whatever your gift is, God wants you to use it—to help others and to show them that He is Lord.

IN JOPPA THERE LIVED A GOOD WOMAN NAMED TABITHA, WHO WAS A FOLLOWER OF JESUS. SHE LOVED TO HELP PEOPLE AND GIVE MONEY TO THOSE IN NEED, AND SHE MADE CLOTHES FOR THE POOR.

BUT SADLY, TABITHA BECAME ILL AND DIED. WHEN HER FRIENDS LEARNED THAT PETER WAS PREACHING NEARBY, THEY BEGGED HIM TO COME AND HELP.

PLEASE HELP, PETER!

ALSO KNOWN AS: DORCAS

WHERE: THE CITY OF JOPPA, IN ISRAEL

KNOWN FOR: ALWAYS DOING GOOD AND HELPING THE POOR

God has given each of you a gift from his great variety of spiritual gifts. Use them well to serve one another.
—1 PETER 4:10 NLT

188

Tabitha had a spiritual gift. She was good at giving, and she used her gift to help the poor. In Joppa, she was well known for all the good she did.

But one day Tabitha became sick and died. The people heard that Peter was in a nearby town, and they sent word for him to come. When he arrived, Peter was taken upstairs to the room where Tabitha lay. Crowding around Peter, the widows cried as they showed him the clothes Tabitha had made for them.

Peter sent everyone out, and he got down on his knees and prayed. Then, turning to the dead woman, Peter said, "Tabitha, stand up!" She opened her eyes and sat up! Peter called for the others to come and see. Many people believed in Jesus because of this miracle.

Tabitha had a gift for giving. Peter had a gift of healing by the Holy Spirit's power. Both of them were willing to use their gifts. And both changed many lives by doing so. No gift is bigger or greater than any other. All are given by God. Use your gift to serve God today. ▶Acts 9

🏃 HERO TRAINING It's easy to look at the gift someone else has and think that it's better than your gift. Read 1 Corinthians 12:4–11. Does everyone have a gift? Is any one gift better than another? Who is the Giver of these gifts?

🦸 BE A HERO!

If you've given your life to God, then you have a spiritual gift too. You just need to discover it. Ask your parents or a leader at church to help you find a spiritual gift test. Then start using that gift!

Who's Knocking?

Peter—The Free

HEROD PUT PETER IN PRISON AND UNDER GUARD OF FOUR SQUADS OF SOLDIERS. DURING THE NIGHT, AN ANGEL VISITED.

"Playing to the crowd" means doing whatever will make the crowd happy. Sometimes it's harmless, like telling funny jokes. Other times it's hurtful, like making fun of someone. In the case of King Herod, playing to the crowd was downright deadly.

First, Herod arrested members of the church. Then he had James, the brother of John, killed. When that made the Jews happy, Herod arrested Peter. Peter's situation seemed hopeless. But the church was praying.

The night before his trial, Peter slept chained between two soldiers. Suddenly an angel appeared, and the chains fell away. Peter followed the angel past the guards and out of the prison. Just as suddenly, the angel disappeared.

WHO: PETER AND KING HEROD AGRIPPA I

WHERE: JERUSALEM

DID YOU KNOW? KING HEROD AGRIPPA I WAS THE GRANDSON OF HEROD THE GREAT, WHO TRIED TO KILL JESUS AS A BABY. HE WAS THE NEPHEW OF HEROD ANTIPAS, WHO KILLED JOHN THE BAPTIST AND WAS PART OF JESUS' TRIAL.

"With man this is impossible, but with God all things are possible."
—MATTHEW 19:26 NIV

Peter went to the house where the church was praying for him and knocked. A servant named Rhoda came to the door and recognized Peter's voice on the other side. She was so excited that she ran back to tell the others, completely forgetting to let Peter in!

The people inside the house didn't believe that Peter was outside. "You're out of your mind," they told Rhoda. "It must be his angel." But Peter kept knocking. At last they opened the door—and there stood Peter!

Even though the believers had been praying, they were surprised by Peter's escape.

🐱 BE A HERO!

Those in prison aren't the only ones who struggle—their families do too. Many prisons have Angel Trees for kids whose parents are in prison. Ask your parents to help you adopt a child for Christmas—or start an Angel Tree ministry for your local prison. Find out more at www.prisonfellowship.org /about/angel-tree.

They forgot that, with God, anything is possible. When you're in a tough situation, don't give up. Pray. And believe that God can make the impossible possible. ▶ACTS 12

🏃 HERO TRAINING Things did not end well for King Herod. Read Acts 12:21–23. What did he do that angered God? Why did it anger God? What was his punishment?

PETER DID AS THE ANGEL INSTRUCTED AND FOLLOWED HIM OUT PAST THE SLEEPING GUARDS.

In a Whole New Light

Saul—The Changed

Have you ever heard anyone say, "He has a heart of stone"? It means a person doesn't allow himself to feel love or kindness or compassion for others. When it came to Christians, Saul's heart was as cold and hard as stone.

Saul followed all the Jewish laws. And he wanted to make sure everyone else did too. That's why Saul set out to destroy the Christian church; he thought Christians were changing the law. All throughout Jerusalem, he went from house to house, dragging off believers and throwing them in prison. When that wasn't enough, Saul got permission to go to Damascus and do the same thing there.

SAUL! WHY ARE YOU PERSECUTING ME?

AS SAUL NEARED THE CITY, A BRIGHT LIGHT SHONE DOWN. THE LIGHT BLINDED HIM, AND HE FELL TO THE GROUND. AT THAT MOMENT, SAUL HEARD A VOICE.

JOBS: TENTMAKER AND PHARISEE

ALSO KNOWN AS: PAUL

WHERE: ON THE ROAD TO DAMASCUS, A CITY ABOUT 150 MILES FROM JERUSALEM

"I will give you a new heart, and I will put a new spirit in you. I will take out your stony, stubborn heart and give you a tender, responsive heart."
—EZEKIEL 36:26 NLT

Along the way, though, Saul was blinded by a bright light. A voice from heaven called out, "Saul, Saul, why do you persecute Me?" When Saul asked who was speaking, the voice answered, "Jesus." Saul, now completely blind, was led into Damascus.

For three days, Saul didn't eat or drink. Then God sent a man named Ananias to help him. Ananias placed his hands on Saul, and instantly scales fell from Saul's eyes—he could see again. At once, he got up and was baptized.

BE A HERO!

The light of Jesus stopped sinful Saul in his tracks and changed his life. The light of Jesus shining through you can help others change too. Don't be afraid to shine your light (Matthew 5:16). Be kind, do good, help others. Heroes light up the darkness with Jesus' love.

Saul was completely changed. He had hated Jesus so much that he had tried to wipe out His followers. But from then on, he loved Jesus so much that he was willing to die to tell people about Him. Never doubt that God has the power to soften even the hardest of hearts—whether it's your own or the heart of a "Saul" in your life. ▶ACTS 9

🏃 HERO TRAINING When you decide to follow Jesus, you become a new creation. You leave your old, sinful ways behind (2 Corinthians 5:17). But that doesn't mean you won't ever sin again. When you mess up, don't give up. Read Philippians 1:6 and remember that God's not finished with you yet!

An Open Heart

Lydia—Who Heard

PAUL AND SILAS WENT TO PHILIPPI. ON THE SABBATH, THEY SHARED THE GOOD NEWS WITH THE WOMEN OUTSIDE THE CITY GATE.

JOB: BUSINESSWOMAN; SOLD PURPLE CLOTH

WHERE: PHILIPPI, A CITY IN MACEDONIA

DID YOU KNOW? IN BIBLE TIMES, PURPLE CLOTH WAS COSTLY AND ONLY WORN BY THE VERY RICH.

"You will search for me. And when you search for me with all your heart, you will find me!"

—JEREMIAH 29:13 ICB

194

Things can be opened to take something out or to put something in—or both. Jars open, doors open, and books open. But did you know that hearts and minds can open too? When we turn to God, seeking to truly worship Him, He opens our hearts and minds. He takes out the things of this world that don't belong and puts in an understanding of Him. And often He uses other believers to help Him do that.

That's what happened with Paul and Lydia. Because there were not enough Jewish people in Philippi to have a synagogue, the worshippers of God gathered outside the city by the river. When Paul arrived in Philippi, he went to the river to tell them about Jesus.

One of the women listening was named Lydia. She was a businesswoman who sold purple cloth. But more importantly, she was a worshipper of God. When Paul began to speak, the Lord opened Lydia's heart. She believed the truth about God and Jesus. Then she was baptized.

Some people long to worship God, but they aren't sure how or where to start. That's where you come in. Tell them about Jesus and pray that God opens their hearts and minds to hear His truth. ▶ACTS 16

♦ BE A HERO!

Jesus often taught by water. While there's nothing magical about water, it is wonderful to worship God outside in His creation. Whether it's by a fountain, a stream, a river, or just the sprinklers, gather your friends or family to read, pray, and praise God near the water.

🏃 **HERO TRAINING** To help you better understand God's Word, use a study Bible with notes and look up verses in different translations. And always pray for God's Spirit to open your heart and mind to His Word (John 14:26).

LYDIA BELIEVED AND WANTED TO BE BAPTIZED. PAUL BAPTIZED HER AND HER WHOLE HOUSEHOLD.

Praise in the Dark
Paul and Silas—The Prisoners

Imagine you've been arrested, beaten, and then chained in a prison cell. What would you do? Cry? Wail? Moan? That would certainly be understandable. But would you sing? Probably not, you say? Well, that's exactly what Paul and Silas did after their arrest in Philippi.

After being falsely accused of teaching against Roman law, Paul and Silas were beaten and chained to a prison wall. It was about midnight, and they were praying and singing to God.

Suddenly a violent earthquake shook the prison. The doors flew open, and every prisoner's chains dropped away. When the jailer woke, he thought everyone had escaped. He was very

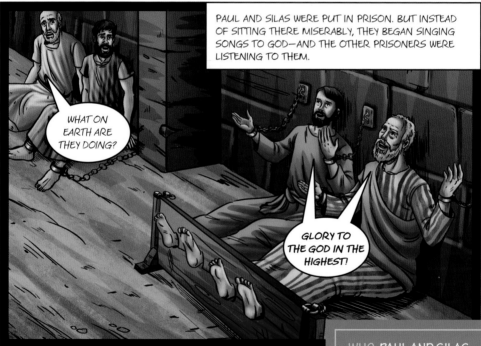

PAUL AND SILAS WERE PUT IN PRISON. BUT INSTEAD OF SITTING THERE MISERABLY, THEY BEGAN SINGING SONGS TO GOD—AND THE OTHER PRISONERS WERE LISTENING TO THEM.

WHAT ON EARTH ARE THEY DOING?

GLORY TO THE GOD IN THE HIGHEST!

WHO: PAUL AND SILAS (A JERUSALEM CHURCH LEADER WHO TRAVELED WITH PAUL ON HIS SECOND MISSIONARY JOURNEY)

WHERE: PHILIPPI, A CITY IN MACEDONIA

My brothers and sisters, when you have many kinds of troubles, you should be full of joy.
—JAMES 1:2 NCV

THAT NIGHT AN EARTH-QUAKE SHOOK THE PRISON, OPENING THE ENTRANCE.

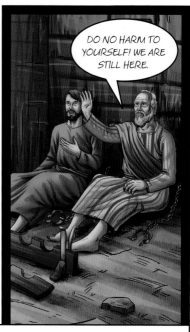

DO NO HARM TO YOURSELF! WE ARE STILL HERE.

CONVINCED THAT PAUL AND SILAS HAD ESCAPED, THE JAILER DREW HIS SWORD TO KILL HIMSELF. HE HEARD PAUL CALL OUT, AND WALKED INSIDE THE CELL TO SEE THAT PAUL AND SILAS WERE STILL INSIDE.

upset because he knew he would be punished for losing prisoners. But Paul called out, "We're all here!"

Relieved and amazed, the jailer fell trembling before Paul and Silas. "Sirs, what must I do to be saved?" he asked.

They answered, "Believe in Jesus." That very night the jailer and all his household were baptized. He was filled with joy because he had come to believe in God.

It's easy to praise God when everything is going your way. It's not so easy when everything is going wrong. But whether the sun is shining on your life or an earthquake of trouble is rattling your world, God is always worthy of your praise. ▶ACTS 16

🏃 HERO TRAINING James 1:2 tells us to be full of joy—even when suffering. How is that possible? By remembering that suffering can actually make us better followers of God. Read Romans 5:3–5 to find out how.

🦸 BE A HERO!

Praising God has the power to ease suffering by reminding us of His goodness and power. And when we put that praise to music, it becomes even more powerful. Ephesians 5:19 commands us to sing and make music in our hearts. So like Paul and Silas, sing a song of praise—even in unlikely places.

Sharing Jesus

Priscilla and Aquila—Missionaries at Home

WE WOULD BE HONORED IF YOU WOULD STAY WITH US, PAUL.

PAUL WENT TO CORINTH AND STAYED WITH AQUILA AND PRISCILLA. THEY WERE HAPPY TO SUPPORT HIS MISSION TO SHARE THE GOSPEL.

JOB: TENTMAKERS, JUST LIKE PAUL

WHERE: THE CITY OF EPHESUS, IN MODERN TURKEY

DID YOU KNOW? PRISCILLA AND AQUILA MET PAUL IN CORINTH. WHEN PAUL WENT TO EPHESUS, PRISCILLA AND AQUILA FOLLOWED HIM.

Jesus said to his followers, "Go everywhere in the world, and tell the Good News to everyone."
—MARK 16:15 NCV

What do you think of when you hear the word *missionary*? Maybe it's someone who travels deep into the wilderness to share Jesus with people who've never heard of Him. Or perhaps it's someone learning a new language so he or she can share Jesus in another country.

While both those ideas are true, being a missionary can also be a lot simpler. A missionary is simply someone who shares the truth about God and His Son, Jesus.

Paul was a missionary. And when he was in Corinth, he met Priscilla and Aquila who welcomed him into their home. They wanted to support his missionary work. And later when they lived in Ephesus, they did some missionary work of their own. One day they heard a man named Apollos speak. Apollos knew the Scriptures. And the things he taught about Jesus were true. But he didn't know the full truth about Jesus as the Messiah.

Priscilla and Aquila invited Apollos to their home. There, they shared the full truth about Jesus and the Holy Spirit. Apollos believed, and he went on to teach many people the full truth about Jesus, the Son of God.

Priscilla and Aquila didn't travel across the world. They didn't learn a foreign language. They simply invited someone into their home to teach about Jesus. So don't let big ideas about the word *missionary* scare you away. You can be a missionary too. Just tell someone about Jesus today. ▶ ACTS 18

🏃 HERO TRAINING When you want to tell someone about God, where do you start? Psalm 96:3 shares a good idea. Tell of all the wonderful things God has done. Share God's work in nature, in the lives of His Bible heroes, and in your own life too.

AQUILA AND PRISCILLA HEARD APOLLOS PREACH ABOUT JESUS. THEY INVITED HIM INTO THEIR HOME.

WELCOME, APOLLOS!

PLEASE COME IN.

The Things That Last

Paul—Who Learned to Love

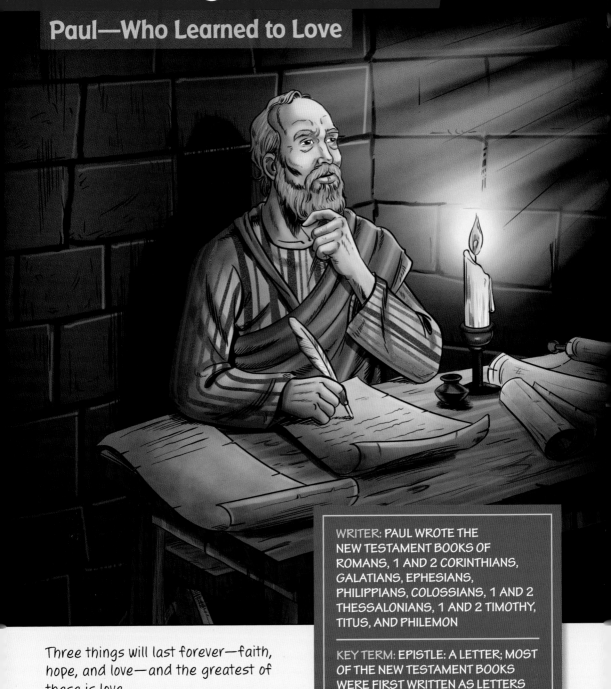

WRITER: PAUL WROTE THE NEW TESTAMENT BOOKS OF ROMANS, 1 AND 2 CORINTHIANS, GALATIANS, EPHESIANS, PHILIPPIANS, COLOSSIANS, 1 AND 2 THESSALONIANS, 1 AND 2 TIMOTHY, TITUS, AND PHILEMON

KEY TERM: EPISTLE: A LETTER; MOST OF THE NEW TESTAMENT BOOKS WERE FIRST WRITTEN AS LETTERS

Three things will last forever—faith, hope, and love—and the greatest of these is love.

—1 CORINTHIANS 13:13 NLT

I f you need to tell someone something, what do you do? Do you pick up the phone? Maybe you send a text. You probably don't send a letter, but letters used to be the only way to share news. In fact, most of the books of the New Testament were originally written as letters to share the good news of Jesus.

Paul wrote several of those letters. He wrote to those he met on his travels. He wrote to many of the churches he helped start. He wrote to his fellow teachers. His letters were filled with advice and corrections, encouragement and love.

Paul's letters were inspired by God, and they still have meaning for us today. So when he wrote that it's faith in Jesus that saves us, it's still true. And when he urged people to put on the armor of God, that's true too. Paul's letters to Timothy encouraged him not to back down from his faith because he was young. That's good advice for you today!

One of Paul's most beautiful letters was written to the Corinthians. It reminded them that faith in God, hope in His promises, and love are the things that last. And love is the greatest of all these things because God Himself is love.

It doesn't matter whether you send letters or text messages. What does matter is that you tell people how much they are loved by the One who made them and gave them His Word. ▶ GALATIANS 2 AND 6; 1 TIMOTHY 4; 1 CORINTHIANS 13

🏃 BE A HERO!

Sometimes our world says it's not cool to show love—not to your parents, not to your brothers or sisters, not to your friends. Don't believe it! Real heroes aren't afraid to show their love. You can love your friends by writing them encouraging notes. You can love your parents by obeying them. And when you think of it, say, "I love you!"

PAUL'S LETTER TAUGHT THAT THE MOST IMPORTANT THING IS TO SHOW LOVE.

🏃 HERO TRAINING One of the most beautiful descriptions of love is found in 1 Corinthians 13:4–7. Read it out loud. Try out a few different translations. Insert God's name in place of the word love to see how much He loves you. Then insert your name in place of the word love to see how you should love others.

He Is Coming!

John—Who Saw Heaven

When someone you love is coming for a visit, you get ready. You tidy your room, put on your best clothes, and put out snacks.

Jesus wants you to get ready for Him. He's coming back—not to visit but to take His followers home to heaven. So He wants your heart and soul to be ready. That's why Jesus gave His disciple John a glimpse of what will happen when He returns.

John was a prisoner on Patmos when Jesus suddenly appeared in a vision. Jesus' hair was pure white, and His eyes blazed like fire. "Do not be afraid," He said. "Write down everything you see."

First, Jesus gave John messages for seven churches. Then John saw a door in heaven open. Looking beyond the door, he saw a huge throne. Surrounding it were twenty-four

DO NOT BE AFRAID. I AM THE FIRST AND LAST.

JOHN SAW A FIGURE LIKE THE SON OF MAN, WITH PURE WHITE HAIR AND EYES LIKE BLAZING FIRE. HE WAS STANDING AMONG SEVEN GOLDEN LAMPSTANDS AND HELD SEVEN STARS IN HIS HAND.

BROTHER: JAMES

AGE: 80 TO 90 YEARS OLD

WHERE: ON THE GREEK ISLAND OF PATMOS, WHERE JOHN WAS IMPRISONED FOR TEACHING ABOUT JESUS

DID YOU KNOW? THE BOOK OF REVELATION IS THE ONLY PROPHETIC BOOK OF THE NEW TESTAMENT.

"After I go and prepare a place for you, I will come back. Then I will take you to be with me so that you may be where I am."
—JOHN 14:3 ICB

other thrones, each with an elder sitting on it. John next saw the coming battle between good and evil. He saw Satan cast into a lake of fire. After that, John was given a look into the Holy City of God, shining with the glory of God. Then Jesus called out, "I am coming soon!"

Jesus will return to earth but not when anyone expects Him (1 Thessalonians 5:2; Mark 13:32). But God's heroes aren't worried. If you've put your faith in God, then you're ready. Now help everyone else to be ready too! ▶THE BOOK OF REVELATION

🦸 BE A HERO!

Jesus has a place prepared for you in heaven. Why not prepare a place for Him on earth? Clear out a corner of your room, a spot under the tree, or any place you like to be. Use it for your quiet time with Jesus. Heroes prepare a place for Jesus in their lives.

🦸 HERO TRAINING John 14:2–3 promises that Jesus has gone on to heaven to prepare a place for His followers. What does 1 Corinthians 2:9 tell you about this place? What do you think you will love most about heaven?

THE HOLY CITY SHONE WITH THE GLORY OF GOD. ITS TEMPLE WAS THE LORD GOD ALMIGHTY AND THE LAMB. THE RIVER OF LIFE RAN THROUGH ITS CENTER. THE CITY HAD NO NEED FOR THE SUN OR THE MOON, BECAUSE THE GLORY OF GOD SHONE ON IT, AND THE LAMB WAS ITS LAMP.

I AM COMING SOON!

AMEN. COME, LORD JESUS!

What Happened When?

CREATION
DATES UNKNOWN

THE STORIES IN THE BIBLE TAKE PLACE OVER MANY CENTURIES. IT IS HARD TO KNOW THE EXACT DATES OR LOCATIONS OF KEY EVENTS. HERE IS A TIMELINE OF FAMOUS BIBLE STORIES, THEIR LOCATIONS, AND ESTIMATES OF WHEN THEY HAPPENED! (ALL DATES ARE APPROXIMATE.)

NOAH SURVIVES
THE GREAT FLOOD
BEFORE 2500 BC

SOLOMON BUILDS
THE TEMPLE
960 BC

ABRAHAM IS BORN
1996 BC

SODOM IS DESTROYED
1897 BC

DAVID IS KING
OF ISRAEL
1010 BC

DEATH OF SAUL
1010 BC

JACOB AND ESAU ARE BORN
1837 BC

MOSES IS BORN
1530 BC

THE ISRAELITES
LEAVE EGYPT
1491 BC

GOD GIVES MOSES
THE TEN
COMMANDMENTS
1491 BC

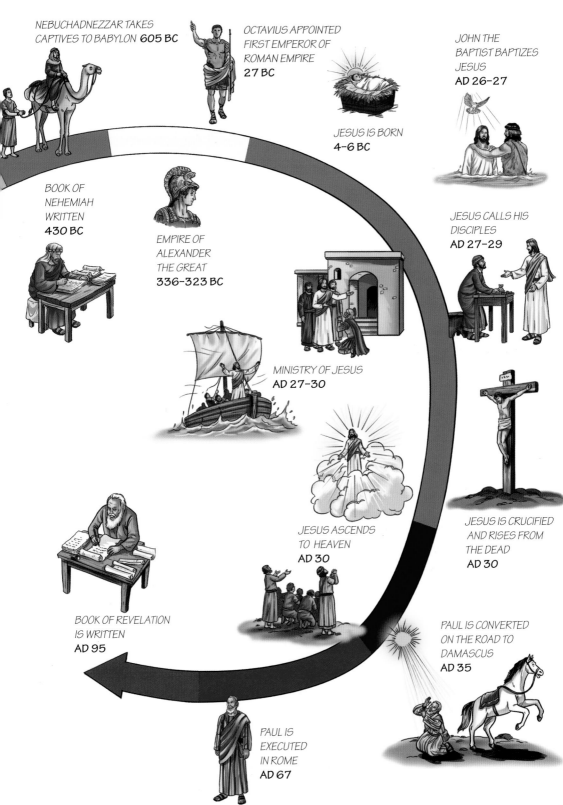

NEBUCHADNEZZAR TAKES CAPTIVES TO BABYLON **605 BC**

OCTAVIUS APPOINTED FIRST EMPEROR OF ROMAN EMPIRE **27 BC**

JOHN THE BAPTIST BAPTIZES JESUS **AD 26-27**

JESUS IS BORN **4-6 BC**

BOOK OF NEHEMIAH WRITTEN **430 BC**

EMPIRE OF ALEXANDER THE GREAT **336-323 BC**

JESUS CALLS HIS DISCIPLES **AD 27-29**

MINISTRY OF JESUS **AD 27-30**

JESUS ASCENDS TO HEAVEN **AD 30**

JESUS IS CRUCIFIED AND RISES FROM THE DEAD **AD 30**

BOOK OF REVELATION IS WRITTEN **AD 95**

PAUL IS CONVERTED ON THE ROAD TO DAMASCUS **AD 35**

PAUL IS EXECUTED IN ROME **AD 67**

The World of the Bible

DACIA

ILLYRICUM

THRACE

Rome

ITALY

Adriatic
Sea

MACEDONIA

Philippi

Nicopolis

Aegean
Sea

AS

SICILY

Corinth

Patmos

Ephesus

LYC

CRETE

Mediterranean Sea

AFRICA

LIBYA

Sahara Desert